ARABIC   ASTRONOMY   ...OGY
GANISATION   CALCULUS   ...TRY
COMMERCIAL CORRESPONDENC... TO
OKING   CRICKET   DRAWING   DRESSMAKING   ...TON
ELECTRICITY IN THE HOUSE   ELOCUTIONIST   EMBROIDERY
ENGLISH RENASCENCE TO THE ROMANTIC REVIVAL   ROMANTIC
EVERYDAY FRENCH   TO EXPRESS YOURSELF   FISHING   TO FLY
ASE BOOK   GARDENING   GAS IN THE HOUSE   GEOGRAPHY OF
IONARY   GERMAN GRAMMAR   GERMAN PHRASE BOOK   GOLF
GOOD FARM ACCOUNTING   GOOD FARM CROPS   GOOD FARMING
UIT FARMING   GOOD GRASSLAND   GOOD AND HEALTHY ANIMALS
GOOD POULTRY KEEPING   GOOD SHEEP FARMING   GOOD SOIL
BLE   HINDUSTANI   HISTORY: ABRAHAM LINCOLN ALEXANDER THE
EAU CONSTANTINE COOK CRANMER ERASMUS GLADSTONE AND
MILTON PERICLES PETER THE GREAT PUSHKIN RALEIGH RICHELIEU
ODROW   ...   .NURSING   ...SE MANA...EMENT
ALIAN   ...   ...   LETTER
ENGIN...   ...ANICS
ODERN   ...ORING
PHILOSO...   ...YSIC
PLUMBI...   PUBLIC
RECKO...   USSIAN

... AND HE WILL BE
YET WISER *Proverbs 9·9*

K: ITS N... ...D PURPOSE   SOCCER   SPANISH   SPE...   AND
SWA... SWEDISH   TEACHING   THINKING   TRIG... METRY
BRI...H RAILWAYS FOR BOYS   CAMPING FOR BOYS AND GIRLS
FOR GIRLS   MODELMAKING FOR BOYS   NEEDLEWORK FOR GIRLS
BOYS AND GIRLS   SAILING AND SMALL BOATS FOR BOYS AND GIRLS
ORK FOR BOYS   ADVERTISING & PUBLICITY   ALGEBRA   AMATEUR
PING   BIOLOGY   BOOK-KEEPING   BRICKWORK   BRINGING UP
NTRY   CHEMISTRY   CHESS   CHINESE   COMMERCIAL ARITHMETIC
TRAVELLING   TO COMPOSE MUSIC   CONSTRUCTIONAL DETAILS
NG   DUTCH   DUTTON SPEEDWORDS   ECONOMIC GEOGRAPHY
ST   EMBROIDERY   ENGLISH GRAMMAR   LITERARY APPRECIATION
IVAL   ROMANTIC REVIVAL   VICTORIAN AGE   CONTEMPORARY
FISHING   TO FLY   FREELANCE WRITING   FRENCH   FRENCH
OUSE   GEOGRAPHY OF LIVING THINGS   GEOLOGY   GEOMETRY
ASE BOOK   GOLF   GOOD CONTROL OF INSECT PESTS   GOOD
FARM CROPS   GOOD FARMING   GOOD FARMING BY MACHINE
ND   GOOD AND HEALTHY ANIMALS   GOOD MARKET GARDENING
GOOD SHEEP FARMING   GOOD SOIL   GOOD ENGLISH   GREEK
ORY: ABRAHAM LINCOLN ALEXANDER THE GREAT BOLIVAR BOTHA
CRANMER ERASMUS GLADSTONE AND LIBERALISM HENRY V JOAN OF
EAT PUSHKIN RALEIGH RICHELIEU ROBESPIERRE THOMAS JEFFERSON
HOME NURSING   HORSE MANAGEMENT   HOUSEHOLD DOCTOR
OURNALISM   LATIN   LAWN TENNIS   LETTER WRITER   MALAY
PONENTS   WORKSHOP PRACTICE   MECHANICS   MECHANICAL
MORE GERMAN MOTHERCRAFT   MOTORING   MOTOR CYCLING
APHY   PHYSICAL GEOGRAPHY   PHYSICS   PHYSIOLOGY   PITMAN
UESE   PSYCHOLOGY   PUBLIC ADMINISTRATION   PUBLIC SPEAKING

THE TEACH YOURSELF BOOKS
EDITED BY LEONARD CUTTS

DICTIONARY OF ANTIQUES

THE TEACH YOURSELF BOOKS

DICTIONARY OF
ANTIQUES

ERNLE BRADFORD

THE ENGLISH UNIVERSITIES PRESS LTD
102 NEWGATE STREET
LONDON E.C.1

First printed 1963

Copyright © 1963
The English Universities Press Ltd

Made and printed in Great Britain for the English Universities Press Ltd.
by Butler & Tanner Ltd., Frome and London

PREFACE

The subject of antiques and antique-collecting attracts more and more people at this present day. It is no longer only the connoisseur or wealthy collector who takes an interest in the masterpieces of art and craftsmanship of the past. Not to put too fine a point on it, nowadays almost everyone is a collector—whether of wool-pictures, steel engravings, Victoriana, Staffordshire pottery, or Regency furniture.

This Dictionary has been designed with the interests of the ordinary collector in mind, and with the hope that it will provide an answer to those questions of names, dates, and provenance which inevitably occur in any discussion of antiques. Most of the entries refer to articles made prior to 1830, since this is the date accepted by the British Antique Dealers' Association as marking the division between what is truly acceptable as an antique, and what is no more than 'old'. At the same time, wherever it seemed right and proper, the Victorian era has not been forgotten.

The Dictionary is not intended to be an essential companion of *Teach Yourself Antiques* in this series. But it has been designed to be complementary to the subjects discussed in that volume. Similarly, the line drawings in the Dictionary, like the line drawings in *Teach Yourself Antiques*, are intended to elucidate those points of detail which are not easy to describe in words. Finally, I should like to place on record my thanks to my wife for her invaluable assistance in the long task of collecting and collating the material for this Dictionary.

E. B.
1963

A

Aaron's rod
A straight moulding of rounded section. Floral leafage or scroll-work is shown emerging from the end of the moulding. The term is also used to denote a wand or rod with a serpent twined around it.

Abruzzi ware
Majolica or tin-enamelled ware, produced by the lesser-known Italian factories. A characteristic of this type of pottery is its warm colours which were made with a tin or lead composition. (See Majolica.)

Acacia
This wood was very popular for marquetry work. It has a yellowish colour with brown veins. It was widely used by the 18th-century cabinet-makers, sometimes in place of the rarer tulip-wood.

Acanthus
This name was given by the Greeks and Romans to a genus of plants, especially Bear's Breech. The attractive shape of the leaves led to the use of acanthus in art.
A conventional representation of the leaf was used in the Corinthian and Composite Orders of Architecture. In the 17th and 18th centuries the acanthus leaf became a favourite motif with wood-carvers. In the mid- and late 18th century it was often used as a decoration on the edge of chair seats.

Acanthus swags
Small rosettes or carved paterae usually oval or round. They embodied the acanthus leaf motif. Adam and Sheraton designs of furniture often made use of these acanthus swags. (See Patera.)

Acorn-turning
Jacobean chair ornaments, resembling acorns. They were often used as finials at the top of chair-backs.

Adam period
Derives its name from the brothers Adam, architects and designers (see Appendix I), active in the latter half of the 18th century. The period or style was based on Roman designs and motifs and is closely related to the Neo-Classic.

Adams
An early Staffordshire factory which specialised in jasper-ware, Egyptian black, and a number of stonewares.

Agate ware
An earthenware made to resemble veined agate.

Aigrette
A hair ornament, in the form of a spray or plume, usually of gold or silver set with pearls or gemstones.

Albert
A gold chain for a man's watch, called after the Prince Consort.

Alder
A wood used in chair-making, but not of the best quality. A dark yellowish colour, the wood is native to England, and its bark is also used for dying articles.

Almery
Another form of the word ambry (q.v.). It was used in churches in the Middle Ages for the receipt of alms. In its later development it became the repository for the chalice and other sacred articles and vessels.

Amaranth
A hardwood obtained from British Guiana. (See Purple Heart.)

Amboyna
Marquetry and veneering timber of rich brown colour and

often 'bird's-eyed'. It comes from the East Indies, and was used in the 18th century largely for furniture panelling.

Ambry
A small cupboard used in churches for holding alms before distribution. It was also used for the storage of ecclesiastical vessels and utensils. The term is also sometimes applied to a recess in a church wall which was sealed off by a door.

Amorini
Cherubs and cupids often found as decoration on furniture of the Renaissance period. During the 17th and 18th centuries in England amorini were popular with wood-carvers and furniture makers, particularly for pieces of a baroque and opulent nature.

Amphora
A Greek vase-shaped vessel with two handles. The standard vessel of antiquity for holding wine, oil etc., it had a capacity of 5 gallons and over. Considerable quantities of amphorae have been discovered by divers in the Mediterranean in recent years. Made of earthenware, most amphorae were undecorated, practical objects, although the amphora shape was also used for household urns which, on occasions, were painted and inscribed.

Andirons—or Fire-dogs
These metal supports for logs on hearth usually had two feet in front and one at back. Until the beginning of 15th century they were made of wrought iron. Most andirons after this date were made of cast iron, but by the 18th century they were being made of steel. Early andirons were simple in design, but in the 18th century they were often as carefully and elaborately designed as the other hearth furniture and decorations of the rooms.

Angel mark
A mark found on Continental pewter which indicated that it was of the highest quality.

Annealing
Toughening and softening metal by heating to make it malleable.

Anthemion
The Grecian honeysuckle. This was a very popular motif with the wood-carver and the inlayer. It will be found quite commonly in late 18th century work and was sometimes used by the Adam Brothers as well as by Sheraton.

Apostle spoons
These are sets of thirteen spoons, usually of silver, whose handles are formed by the figures of the Apostles. Very few complete early sets exist, although they have been widely imitated in succeeding centuries. They were particularly popular in the 16th century.

Apple
This wood was used in country furniture, particularly in 17th and 18th centuries. Never a high-grade furniture wood, it will not be found in the work of the London and best provincial woodworkers and cabinet-makers.

Applied mouldings
Sometimes called Jacobean ornament, this was a type of moulding applied to furniture to simulate the effect of panelling. It was mostly used in the 17th century.

Appliqué
Appliqué designs in furniture are patterns such as fret-cut work glued or otherwise applied to the main body of the article. In textiles they are designs of a different material to the basic fabric which are sewn on at a later date from the initial weave.

Apron
Sometimes called a skirting piece, this was a supporting piece of timber between the seat framing of a chair, or beneath the edge of a table. Also the base between the feet of a cabinet. The apron did not always give structural support,

but was sometimes no more than a masking piece to conceal the construction.

Aquila

A lectern or reading desk used in churches. From the Latin 'aquila', 'an eagle', since it usually takes this form. Most commonly made of brass although aquilas have also been made in wood and silver.

Arabesque

An Oriental design, most probably reaching Europe from the Moorish occupation of Spain. It usually consists of floral and foliage motifs elaborately intertwined. In woodcarving, arabesques are usually in low relief. The term is also loosely used for any kind of scroll-work.

Arcading

A type of ornament or design found in woodwork which consists of a gallery or row of arches which resembles an architectural arcade.

Argyle

A tureen with a spout used for gravy. It has an outer container into which hot water is poured to keep the gravy hot. Late 18th century, and supposedly deriving its name from the Duke of Argyll who has been credited with its invention. Made either in silver or Sheffield plate.

Armchair

The chair with arm-supports came into general use in England during the Tudor period. Its history is much older, for royal thrones had been of the 'armchair' type for thousands of years. The carver and chair-maker reached their peak of excellence during the 18th century, after which the stuffed or upholstered armchair began to supplant the wooden chair.

Armoire

A large cupboard or wardrobe of French design. It is often

decorated with carved panels of flowers and trophies. The term is also applied on the Continent to the ambry (q.v.). Used in the Middle Ages for storing arms and armour, the armoire is the progenitor of the wardrobe.

Arras
Originally a loose-textured tapestry woven at Arras in Flanders. Later the term became synonymous with a curtain or wall-covering, usually with a figure pattern.

Ash
A hard white wood, almost as tough as oak, but of less use in furniture since its long fibrous grain renders it liable to split.

Ashbury metal
A hard type of pewter used for spoons and forks.

Assay
The testing of metals to ensure that they are of a standard fineness. The Goldsmiths' Company at the Goldsmiths' Hall in London received its Charter in 1327, which gave it the power to assay and mark articles of gold and silver.

Astbury
Ware made by John and Thomas Astbury in Staffordshire in the first half of the 18th century. A fine earthenware with a lead glaze, it often had floral decorations in white on a coloured body. Buff, chocolate and red were among the body colours used. Many ornaments and figures were produced in this ware as well as household articles.

Asterism
The six- or twelve-pointed-star effect seen in certain gemstones—usually ruby or sapphire—and visible when they are cut *en cabochon* in the correct direction. Star-stones are also known as 'asterias'.

Astragal
A type of beading fixed to the extreme edge of one of a pair

of doors. After the mid-18th century the term is also applied to the glazing bars in a bookcase or cabinet door. The moulding is usually convex and its main purpose is to prevent dust seeping into bookcases or cabinets.

Aubusson
French town famous for its rugs and tapestry since medieval times. The second half of the 18th century saw the production of much of the finest Aubusson work.

Aventurine
A term found in lacquer work to denote gold dust sprinkled onto a lacquered surface.

Axminster
The English town where the famous carpet factory opened in 1755. Involved designs of interweaved coloured wools of triple chenille texture. After 1835 the factory moved to Wilton.

B

Back stool

A type of upholstered easy-chair without arms and with all four legs alike. As its name suggests, it is basically a stool to which a back has been added. Back stools feature in some of Chippendale's designs.

Bacon cupboard
A cupboard for holding bacon. It sometimes formed the back of a settle. Used in farmhouses in the 17th century and subsequently.

Baguette
A rectangular cut for small diamonds, similar in shape to batons (q.v.) but smaller.

Bail handles
A drop handle suspended from knobs fixed to back plates on drawers and cupboards. In early days bail handles were made of iron, but later of brass and in many patterns.

Balas ruby
A misnomer for red spinel.

Ball flower
A flower-shaped ornament, consisting of a ball held in position by three petals. Popular with carvers and moulding craftsmen as a decoration.

Ball foot
A ball shape used for the foot of furniture. It became popular in the Carolean period but was to some extent superseded by the bracket foot (q.v.). The claw-and-ball foot—with the claw grasping the ball—was introduced from Holland in the late 17th century and was widely used by 18th-century furniture craftsmen and designers, Chippendale among others.

Ball frame
A term used to describe the turned framing of chairs, tables etc. when in the shape of a succession of balls.

Baluster
Usually a turned wood railing found in chair-backs. Also applied to the front of a cupboard for ornamentation. Most commonly found in Elizabethan and Jacobean periods. The baluster may be tapered, or twisted, or vase-shaped.

Baluster (glass)
Stem of glass, slender above and pear-shaped below.

Banding
A strip of inlay which contrasts in colour with the background wood.

Bandy-leg
A name for the cabriole leg, or the leg modelled on an animal form.

Bangle
A bracelet of solid gold, silver, or base metal, but not flexible.

Banister-back
A chair with its back or sides formed of balusters (q.v.).

Banjo-clock
A clock in the shape of the musical instrument, designed for hanging on the wall. The lyre shape was also used. Reputedly invented in America in the early 19th century.

Banner screen
Fashionable in the mid-18th century, these screens had a tapestry or needlework forming a banner, which was on a pole on tripod legs.

Barber's bowl
A bowl with a semi-circle cut out of it to fit the neck when the barber's client was being shaved.

Barbotine
Biscuit and kaolin application to different surfaces.

Barometer
Invented by Toricelli, an Italian, in 17th century. The barometer during the 18th century received the attention of most of the great craftsmen in wood. This meteorological instrument in its early form, the 'stick barometer', worked by measuring the air pressure on a column of mercury. It was superseded in popular use by the aneroid barometers.

Baroque
An ornate style in the arts and crafts reputedly derived from the Portuguese 'barroco'. At its best it is imposing and grand, but at its worst becomes ornament for ornament's sake. Not to be confused with the French 'Rococo', which is more feminine and elegant. Baroque was fashionable in Carolean England and with individual designers at later dates.

Baroque pearls
Irregularly shaped pearls. (Portuguese *barroco*—a rough pearl.)

Basalt
A type of stoneware resembling Egyptian basalt. The most famous use of basalt stoneware was by Wedgwood's factory. It has been little made in the last century.

Bas-relief
A carving in which the figures project from the background, but only to a limited extent. Alto-Relievo or High-Relief is more extreme.

Basse-taille
Also known as translucent enamelling. The design is cut in relief in the metal, and the cavities filled with translucent enamel so that an effect of light and shade is achieved, palest where the high parts of the design are only just covered, deepest at the bases of the cavities.

Basset table
A table made for the game of basset, popular during the reign of Queen Anne. A basset table seats five players.

Batons or Baton cut
A rectangular cut for large diamonds, the rectangle being somewhat elongated.

Battersea enamel
First produced by Stephen Jansen, at Battersea, in 1750. The factory closed in 1756, but the manufacture of these attractive enamels was later carried on at Bilston and elsewhere. The original Battersea enamels are finer and more delicately coloured than their successors. Many types of small decorative objects, toys, snuff boxes and so on were made in this style.

Beaconsfield wardrobe
A type of wardrobe, in which one half is fitted with a hat cupboard and drawers, and the other half serves as a hanging compartment.

Beading
Thin strip of moulding with raised shapes like small beads.

Beaker
A tall cup with no handles. Pewter or silver. Introduced in the early 17th century, the beaker was the forerunner of the modern tumbler.

Beaufait
The original of the modern buffet, this was an oak stand on which food was prepared. Often resembling a court cupboard, it was also used for the storage of food.

Beauvais tapestry
The factory was established in 1664, at Beauvais, in France. The best products of the 18th century sometimes incorporated Boucher designs. Beauvais carpet was a knotted pile carpet made in the late 18th century. In general, Beauvais work was of a popular kind as opposed to the more important work of the Gobelin factory.

Bed
Beginning as a simple mattress or portable couch, the bed evolved into a small separate 'room' of its own—the four-poster. Later, as comfort and carpets prevailed in houses, the bed again became open to the room, and was now considered worthy of decoration and embellishment. Some four-posters were still being made in the 19th century, but, with the advent of comfortable spiral springs and brass bedsteads, the bed rapidly became a manufacturer's rather than a craftsman's object of furniture.

Beech
Although a hardwood, the beech is comparatively 'soft' when compared with oak or ash. It has long been popular with chair-makers, for it is—unlike ash—suitable for turning. Beech has always been used by country craftsmen for chairs. Late 18th-century chairs of the painted type were quite often made of beech.

Beehive chair
Usually made of wicker, it has a tall enclosed back and sides.

Popular in the 19th century, it derives its name from its resemblance to the straw or wicker skep used for beehives.

Belleek

A translucent, ivory-looking porcelain, made in Donegal, from 1857 onwards. This pure white porcelain with its nacreous lustre is often decorated with marine subjects.

Bell flower

A bell-shaped flower used as a chain or pendant. Used as a carved decoration on furniture or in interior decoration.

Bergère

French upholstered, wide-seated armchair of Louis XV Period. It was the original of the modern lounge chair. The original Bergère often has panels made of cane-work.

Berlin

This porcelain factory was established circa 1750 and rose to fame under the patronage of Frederick the Great. It was a hard white pure porcelain, decorated often in blue with floral designs. Household articles and services were made, also decorative figures. After 1760 many workers from the famous Meissen factory were attracted to Berlin, and the work of this factory inevitably became rather similar to that of Meissen. Early marks—a W (for Wegely, the founder), and then a sceptre.

Berlin work

Berlin work or Berlin woolwork became very popular in the mid- and late 19th century. Coloured patterns on squared paper were copied in needlepoint. Much used for covering chair-backs, seats and footstools in the Victorian era.

Bevel

Usually refers to the edge of mirrors and the slant of the mirror at the point where it is set into the frame. Some indication of the age of antique mirrors may be gained by a knowledge of the type of bevelling used at different periods.

Bezel
The groove or flange holding a gemstone in its setting or a watch-glass in place. Also the first four oblique facets of a gemstone cut after the table facet. The term is also applied to the ring or flange holding the glass face of a clock.

Bible box
A lidded box, often made of oak, with incised designs. It was sometimes set on a stand. As its name implies, it was originally intended to hold the family Bible, with its record of births, marriage and deaths.

Biedermeir
A 19th-century German style of furniture. Usually made of cheap woods such as cherry and apple. Metal decorations embellished the furniture, which was sprung and horsehair upholstered.

Bijouterie
The craft of the goldsmith and enameller, as opposed to *joaillerie*, the craft of the mounter and gem-setter. Bijouterie is often used to cover the whole craft of the jeweller, and is sometimes opposed to another French term *minuterie*. The latter is held to be a definition for 'small-work' such as boxes, parasol handles etc.—articles which, strictly, are not 'worn'.

Bilboa mirror
A type of mirror with frame of marble and gilt, surmounted by a double scroll at top. Supposedly originating from Bilboa in Spain.

Billiard table
Invented in France, possibly in the 14th century. The game was being played in England in the Tudor period. The modern style of billiard table did not develop until the 19th century, when many very elaborate examples were made. Some were shown at the Great Exhibition of 1851, with elaborately carved and turned legs and side-decorations in the 'Gothic Style'.

Bilston enamel

A somewhat coarse copy of Battersea enamel (q.v.). The Bilston factory produced a great many enamel boxes, ornaments and toys after 1756 when the Battersea factory was closed. Rather similar work was also produced in other parts of Staffordshire.

Birch

A popular wood with many 18th-century craftsmen. It was often used as a substitute for satinwood, since it has a similar close grain. Like satinwood, birch will take a very fine polish.

Bird-cage clock

Another name for the lantern clock, the universal household clock in the early days of horology. Like the bracket or lantern clock—and its descendant, the long-case clock—it is weight-driven, with the pendulum swinging free below the dial. Popular survivals of the old-fashioned 'bird cage' or lantern clock are the Swiss and German cuckoo clocks.

Biscuit

Pottery that has been fired once and left in an undecorated state. The name derives from the unglazed 'biscuit' colour of the pottery.

Black bean

A golden-coloured Australian hardwood. It is finely figured and has become popular since the 19th century for panelling and other joinery work.

Black wood

A generic name given to a number of hardwoods found in the East and West Indies. All are dark in colour, suitable for some kinds of decorative work, and range from deep, mahogany-brown to an almost port-colour.

Bleeding bowl

A small cup with one or two pierced handles used by surgeons in the past for the operation of 'bleeding' or bloodletting their patients. Made sometimes of silver or of pewter, and often very attractive for their simplicity of design.

Bleeding dish

Similar to above, of silver or pewter, and in use by surgeons from the late 15th century to the 19th.

Blister pearl

Irregularly shaped swellings of nacre, often hollow, within the shell of the pearl-bearing oyster. Much used in 19th-century brooches and pendants.

Blobs

Also known as Seals or Prunts. The small applied 'blobs' of glass used as a decoration to the bowls, stems etc. of glassware.

Block foot

The foot or leg of a piece of furniture which ends in a cube or oblong shape. Taper foot or spade foot are terms used to describe two elegant versions of the basic block foot.

Block-front

The front of a piece of furniture which projects beyond the body or carcass, usually in a rectangular shape—as opposed to bombé, where the shape is swelled and cylindrical.

Body

The clay of which pottery is made. Used also to denote the carcass or basic frame of a piece of furniture.

Bog oak

Oak taken from bogs where it has been preserved and become very dark and almost like coal. In Tudor times, and later, it was popular for inlay work. It had a popular revival in the 19th century, when 'Irish Bog Oak' was used in a number of important exhibition pieces—particularly at the Great Exhibition of 1851.

Bohemian glass

Fine glass of Bohemia. Often of a deep ruby tint, it was made from silicate of potash and lime. Engraved and incised designs in the glass were one of its principal features, and its rich colours gave it a great popularity.

Bolection

A moulding, or all the projecting parts of mouldings. Particularly used with reference to mouldings projecting above the flat surface of panellings.

Boll

A bubble. Any knob-like protuberance on furniture etc. Derived from the rounded seed-vessel of flax and other similar plants.

Bombé

A term applied to articles of Continental furniture, particularly commodes, which swell or bulge out at the front and sides. Much favoured by Dutch designers, but also generally associated with bureaux and commodes of the Louis XIV period. Bombé fronts were copied in England during the William and Mary period of furniture design.

Bone china

A type of porcelain in which bone ash is mixed with kaolin and feldspar. It is whiter than soft-paste, but not so white as hard-paste. It was developed about 1800. The term is often used in England to denote 18th-century porcelain as opposed to pottery.

Bonheur-du-jour

The French term for a particular type of writing table. An elegantly-shaped table, it had a drawer with an adjustable writing slope; the upper and back section having an open centre part with a shelf, on either side of which there was a place for books. It also contained a cupboard, and three drawers, running the whole width, were fitted beneath. These tables were copied by English designers, particularly George Hepplewhite.

Bonnet-top

A scroll or shield-shaped top. Sometimes used of a bonnet-shaped pediment popular in England during the reign of Queen Anne.

Bookcase

Did not really exist as an individual article of furniture until the Jacobean period. Became fashionable after the Restoration of Charles II. Attractive simple types were made during the reign of Queen Anne, but the bookcase *par excellence* did not develop until the 18th century when the nobility were able to commission designers like Chippendale and his contemporaries to make their bookcases worthy of housing their finely-bound libraries. The elegant 'break-front' bookcase with its shelves and drawers beneath also came into fashion during this period.

Bort

Small fragments of diamond, too small for use in jewellery, which are crushed and used as abrasives.

Boss

A rounded or raised projection used as ornament. Of Dutch or Flemish origin, it served to cover the intersections of mouldings.

Boule

The elongated pear-shaped or cylindrical form taken on by the synthetic sapphire, ruby or spinel, during their formation in the Vernueil furnace.

Boulle-work

Tortoiseshell and metal inlay with brass and sometimes silver, and exotic woods. It originated in Italy, but was developed by André Charles Boulle under Louis XIV. The term has been corrupted to 'buhl'. The carcass of a piece of furniture—usually oak or ebony—was covered with tortoiseshell, which in its turn was inlaid with designs in metal. This highly elaborate style of furniture design was almost akin to jewellery in its delicacy and craftsmanship.

Bow

The Bow porcelain factory was established in 1744. It was
the first English manufactory of soft-paste with kaolin.
Tableware and figures were unmarked, or with red anchor
and dagger. The flower painting was very fine. The factory
was bought and removed to Derby by William Duesbury
in 1776. Akin to the porcelain made at Chelsea, the Bow
ware is slightly less fine and not so well executed. Oriental
designs and decorations were copied.

Bow front

A curved smooth front in furniture. It differs from bombé
(q.v.) by being regular in its curve, and not bulged.

Bow top

The curve of the top rail of a chair-back. The curve is
smooth and unbroken between the uprights of the back.

Box bed

A bed that folds up against the wall when not in use. Common formerly in Scotland and the North of England, the
box bed has had a revival of popularity in the small house
and flats of the present day.

Box setting

A closed form of setting where the gemstone is enclosed in
a 'box'. The edges of the metal are pressed down to hold
the stone in place.

Box settle

A box or chest with a hinged lid which forms the seat. In
earliest times the lid was plain wood, but later it was stuffed
or padded.

Box wood

A yellow-coloured timber. It has a particularly small and
regular grain which made it very suitable for use in marquetry work. Box wood has also been used for 'treen' and
other small woodwork.

Bracket
A right-angled support for a shelf or other object. The support between the leg and a piece of furniture. A wall-fitting.

Bracket cornice
A cornice supported by a bracket. Found in examples of the High Renaissance style in Elizabethan and Jacobean furniture.

Bracket foot
A foot, often elaborately decorated, extending in two directions from the base of a piece of furniture. To some extent it superseded the plain ball foot in the Queen Anne period.

Brampton
A type of brown stoneware. Jugs and other domestic articles and ornaments were made of it.

Brass
Copper and zinc alloy, sometimes with tin. Modern brass usually consists of two parts copper with one part zinc. Brassware has been made in England since the reign of Queen Elizabeth I. The term is also used to describe the commemorative sepulchral tablets of brass set in churches.

Brasses
In furniture terms, these include handles and handle-plates. Pear drop handles were the first basic design, then loop handles, and finally the elaborate brasses of the 18th century. Chippendale and other famous furniture designers left designs and patterns for brasses.

Brazil
A hardwood rather similar to mahogany. It is a heavy wood, and is principally used as an inlay.

Breakfast table
An elegant four-legged table, usually associated with Chippendale, and often incorporating a delicate pierced gallery.

Breakfront

A name given to desks, wardrobes, bookcases and side-boards, where a vertical part projects from the main structure. The breakfront became very fashionable in the 18th century, and some of the most elegant pieces of furniture were made in this manner.

Brilliant cut

The best type of cut for the diamond, used also for coloured stones such as zircon. The modern brilliant has a larger table or top facet than the Victorian cut, and has thirty-three facets above the girdle, twenty-five in the base. The brilliant cut was discovered by a Venetian lapidary, Vincenti Peruzzi, in the late 17th century.

Briolette

A pear-shaped drop cut for gemstones. The facets are all triangular.

Bristol and Bristol ware

The Plymouth pottery, where the first hard-paste porcelain was made in England, was transferred to Bristol in 1773. The works closed in 1782. Oriental designs in blue-and-white ware were made at Bristol—domestic services, ornaments, and medallions. There were several marks, among them the letter B, the word 'Bristol' and the letter B with crossed swords. Apart from porcelain, a delft ware was also made in the Bristol potteries during the first half of the 18th century.

Bristol glass

Fine glass was made at Bristol from the 18th century onwards. The coloured glass is well known, as is the valuable opaque white. The Bristol factory began glass manufacture about 1760 and produced a great many domestic articles, as well as toys, decanters, scent bottles etc.

Bristol stone
True 'Bristol stone' is rock-crystal, or colourless quartz.
The term is sometimes erroneously applied to paste, since
Bristol as a glass centre was also a manufacturer of paste
stones for jewellers.

Britannia metal
A type of pewter which contains no lead.

Brocade
A fabric of silk with the design formed by raised metallic
threads, or any material with a similarly raised design.

Broken arch
A type of arch found in 18th-century furniture with opening
at top. This break in the arch was sometimes filled by a
moulding of an urn or similar Classical motif.

Broken pediment
Similar to a broken arch, this is a pediment with the moulding broken for ornamental purposes.
The break occurs at the apex of the
pediment.

Bronze
A copper and tin alloy. The usual percentage is approxi-
mately 8 parts copper to 1 part tin.

Bruiting
The method of roughly fashioning a diamond by rubbing
two diamonds one against the other.

Brussels carpet
Coloured worsted yarns form the design. In the 18th century often a velvet weave uncut. The yarns are woven in
loops on the foundation.

Buckram
Linen or cotton fabric stiffened with gum. Often a coarse
canvas used as a backing in upholstery work.

Buffet
   An antique sideboard. It was used for serving or storing

food. Often an elaborate affair, designed also for the display of plate, it followed many different patterns from simple court cupboard to High Renaissance display furniture. See also Beaufait.

Buhl (see Boulle.)

Bulbous

 Bulb-like. The term is comonly used to describe the bulb-shaped legs of Elizabethan furniture. This bulbous type of leg and support enjoyed a brief return to favour during the 'Gothic Revival' of the 19th century. Usually found in oak furniture, and elaborately carved.

Bullion

Gold or silver before manufacture.

Bun foot

A 17th-century Dutch introduction—shaped like a flattened ball. (See Ball foot.)

Bureau

An enclosed writing cabinet. It derives from a simple box to contain writing materials. This usually had a plain lid and was set on a chest. Later bureaux had pigeon holes, nests of drawers, and fall fronts. Dutch developments of the bureau were brought to England during the William and Mary régime. In France the bureau reached a height of elaboration under Riesener and others. Queen Anne bureaux were usually plain. In the 18th century the bureau gradually became incorporated with the bookcase. A later development was the Victorian davenport (q.v.).

Burl

Figuring of wood with circles and twisted grain forming patterns. Often applied to a form of walnut. Burl is made from the knotted roots of wood where concentric grain and attractive patterning is found.

Burnishing

A process of smoothing carved woodwork so as to give it the

look of modelling. The techinque was popular in the 18th century. The term is also applied to the smoothing of silver and other metals with a burnisher.

Butter cupboard
A type of Jacobean cupboard, perforated for ventilation. Almost invariably made of oak, and with ventilation holes in the front as well as the sides.

Butterfly table
A type of gate-leg table, in which the supports for the drop top are hinged pieces of wood, resembling a butterfly's wing. Reputedly of American design, the butterfly table became quite common in the 19th century.

Button
A fastening for a cupboard or other kind of door. It consists of a piece of wood or metal held by a screw in the centre, which allows it to revolve.

C

Cabinet
A case with glass doors or front for display. Originally it was a cupboard with door above, opening to reveal drawers, and with other drawers below. The china cabinet and the bureau derive from this. The china cabinet as such was introduced mainly to display porcelain. It became a common piece of household furniture in the 19th century when china-collecting became fashionable.

Cabinet-maker
The English equivalent of the French ébéniste. The term is first used at the end of the 17th century. Prior to this date the carpenter and the joiner had made furniture but, with its increasing elaboration, the cabinet-maker became a specialist. The joiner still made country furniture, but in London and the big provincial centres the craft of the 'cabinet-maker' now became established.

Cabochon

The oldest method of cutting gemstones still in use. The top of the stone is rounded, without facets. The base may be concave, convex, or flat. Used mostly for opaque stones, and star-stones. (See Asterism.)

Cabochon moulding

A form of moulding with a rounded surface surrounded by ornamentation. Both in wood and in plaster mouldings, the style called 'cabochon-and-leaf' (a cabochon centre with a foliage surround) was popular in the 18th century.

Cabriole

The word derives from the French 'cabriole'—a goat's 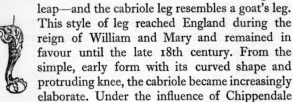 leap—and the cabriole leg resembles a goat's leg. This style of leg reached England during the reign of William and Mary and remained in favour until the late 18th century. From the simple, early form with its curved shape and protruding knee, the cabriole became increasingly elaborate. Under the influence of Chippendale it became heavily decorated with elaborate carving.

Cake basket

Introduced between 1730 and 1750. The silver cake basket gave the craftsman a fine opportunity for the display of his technical ability in pierced work and saw-piercing. Many famous silversmiths, including Paul de Lamerie, made cake baskets. Similar styles of cake baskets with great elaboration (they were die-stamped) were made by the plate manufacturers of Sheffield.

Calamandar

An East Indian hardwood. Hazel-brown in colour with dark streaks, it was much used for small articles.

Cambrian

The name given to various types of ware made at Cambrian Potteries, Swansea, from 1750 onwards. (See Swansea.)

Camel back
A type of chair made fashionable by Hepplewhite with a raised and carved back. More generally known as a shield-back.

Cameo
A carved gem or shell in which the carved design stands out against a darker or lighter background. The carving is in relief, i.e. stands above the background, as opposed to intaglio (q.v.).

Camphor wood
Akin to mahogany in colour and texture, camphor wood comes from Borneo and Kenya. It has been largely used since the 19th century for all chests and chests of drawers intended for the storage of blankets and linen, the odour of camphor attached to the wood making it resistant to moths.

Canapé
A type of divan originating in France large enough to hold several people, and having a high back. An elaboration of this is the canapé confident, a sofa which has also a seat at each end sited at right-angles to the sofa-seat.

Canary wood
A type of light yellowish mahogany. It has been popular since the 18th century for veneering and marquetry work.

Candelabrum
The branched candlestick which became fashionable in the 18th century. Candelabra were made of silver and Sheffield plate, some of the finest work of the platers being found in their matching sets.

Candle snuffer
Originally of iron, and then of brass and silver. The candle snuffer has been used since Tudor times. It was also made in brass and Sheffield plate. Quite often the 'scissors' part of the snuffer is supported on short legs so that it could be laid easily on a tray.

Candlestick
In the early forms the candlestick had a spike at the top
onto which the candle was forced. Such types are still to be
found in some churches. Later, the socket-stick becomes
universal. Early candlesticks were made of brass and pewter;
later examples of silver, Sheffield plate, glass, pottery and
porcelain etc. Carolean silver candlesticks tend to be fluted—
like Classical columns—on plain square bases. Then the
Corinthian-column style became fashionable, and later still
the candlestick became increasingly elaborate with swags
of flowers, classical motifs etc.

Cane
This material is used for the backs and seats of chairs, and
was first introduced at the time of Charles I. It is a feature
of chairs of this period. Cane reached England through
trade with the East, and remained fashionable until the
upholsterer exerted his influence on the furniture-maker in
the reign of William and Mary. Early cane-work (of which
little survives) was coarser in texture than later work.

Canopy chair
A Gothic-type State chair (15th and 16th centuries) which
has a canopy over it. Sometimes called a *Dossier*. Such
chairs, but without the canopy, were sometimes imitated in
the 19th century during the Gothic Revival.

Canted
As applied to parts of furniture, the term means that they
have an inclination off the level; a tilted position.

Canteen
A chest containing sets of cutlery, spoons, forks etc. The
term was also used commonly in the past to denote a cabinet
containing drinks and appropriate glasses.

Canterbury
A supper tray divided in partitions for cutlery and plate,
common during the 18th century. Later the term was also
applied to a small stand divided to hold music.

Capital

The top of a column, distinguished by its Order of Architecture. The five classical orders in architecture are : Tuscan, Doric, Ionic, Corinthian and Composite. Each of these Orders, starting from the short Tuscan, gradually increases in height, delicacy and elaboration.

Capo-di-monte

Porcelain from the factory at Naples established 1736. Originally unmarked, then marked with a fleur-de-lys motif. A soft-paste porcelain of great delicacy.

Caqueteuse

A 16th-century chair. It has a triangular seat, narrow back and spread arms. Later variants were shaped rather like a saddle in the seat, so that the men's coat tails were unencumbered.

Carat

The standard weight used for gemstones, equivalent to one-fifth of a gramme. It is also the measure of fineness of a gold alloy, pure gold being assessed at twenty-four parts. 18-carat gold is commonly used in high-quality jewellery.

Carcase

The main body of a piece of furniture. The most common carcase for English furniture—whatever the veneering or inlay work—has been seasoned oak.

Card-cut

An applied, flat-relief ornament fashionable during the 'Chinese period' of Chippendale.

Card-table

This was introduced in the Carolean period. It became fashionable in the 18th century. Early examples were small, circular, with a gate-leg. Walnut was superseded by mahogany, and in the 18th century the square card-table became almost universal. Many card-tables had the cabriole leg. 'Dishes' for money, counters and drawers for cards were added.

Carlton house

 A type of writing table, made fashionable by Sheraton. The back section is slightly elevated and usually semi-circular. Drawers are fitted in the main part of the table and small drawers in the elevated section.

Carolean

The period of Charles II. Generally taken to include that of James II also. 1660 to 1689. Sometimes also used to cover the period of Charles I.

Carpet

Reputedly introduced into England during the reign of Edward I, they were of Persian origin. Hand-knotted rugs were made in England and France during the 17th century. In early days the term was used to denote any kind of covering, whether of a table or a bed. Carpets did not become general until the 18th century when carpet manufacture began in earnest.

Cartonnier or Cartonnière

A cabinet for filing papers. A small bureau. Invariably fitted with numbers of small drawers—sometimes with secret drawers for the security of money, private papers and other valuables.

Carton pierre

A type of papier mâché or paste and stucco composition. It originated in France but soon became popular in England for elaborations on furniture, panels, ceilings etc. Paper pulp, plaster-of-Paris and glue are the main ingredients. Used considerably during the 19th century for ceiling and skirting ornamentation.

Cartouche

Scroll or carving used ornamentally or with inscription. The scroll terminates in a pleasant curve. The cartouche is quite often found in furniture as well as in interior decoration. On chairs particularly, as on silverware, the cartouche plays the part of a shield.

Carver chair
An American type of chair made of turned work and fitted with a rush seat, called after an original in Pilgrim Hall, Plymouth, said to have been owned by Governor Carver. The Carver chair was also the Victorian name for the two chairs in a dining-room suite which were set at each end of the dining table for the master and mistress of the house.

Carving
Method of decorating wood by chisel or knife. Modelled carving is an elaborate form with the design in high relief. Scratch carving implies the design is cut into the surface. Flat carving merely has the ground cut away from the relief work. In the 19th century hand-carving was almost entirely superseded by machine carving.

Caryatid
Carved female figures derived from classical art. They were greatly used during the Italian Renaissance and, therefore, in Elizabethan furniture. They were revived in fashion during the Classical period of the 18th century, and again in the 19th century, under the Gothic Revival. Male figures used as supporters are known as Atlantes.

Casket
A small chest, usually for jewellery. Caskets have been made in every type of material from wood to gold, silver, Sheffield plate and Bilston enamel.

Cassone
Italian for a chest or coffer. In the Renaissance the designs were very ornate and richly carved. *Caisson*—French for a similar article. *Cassette*—a coffer bound with bands of metal. Used as a jewel and cash chest.

Caster

Early roller-type casters were of wood, and then of brass.

 Silver condiment casters date from the Carolean period. Casters were used both for sugar, pepper and other spices. They were often, though not invariably, made in sets of three. Casters were also made in Sheffield plate during the 18th century. The straight-sided cylindrical caster dates from about 1680. The vase-shaped caster followed about 1700. The octagonal-shaped caster was popular in the Georgian period.

Casting

Shaping of pottery by pouring into moulds. Also used for all types of metal-work from the 18th century onwards. Casting was to some extent supplanted by die-stamping of metal, especially for small articles.

Caudle cup

Caudle was a warm milk drink, flavoured with spices and wine. The caudle cup was usually of silver or pewter, of large proportions and often finely chased. Wider at the bottom than the top, caudle cups usually had two handles. They are found in England from the 17th century onwards.

Caughley

From the factory in Shropshire established c. 1750. It made fine earthenware and then, under Thomas Turner, 1772, soft-paste porcelain, particularly in the 'Willow-pattern'. The factory was sold to John Rose of Coalport in 1799 and remained in operation until 1814. The ware was somewhat similar to that of Worcester (q.v.), enamel painting and transfer printing being used. Marks—the most usual is a C, also the letter S or Salopian for 'Salopian Ware'.

Causeuse

A canapé, or sofa chair, on which two people can sit to talk. The causeuse became popular in England and France in the 19th century.

Cedar
A brown wood used for drawers, linings etc. It has a delicate scent. Cedar is little used for cabinet-work being too light and soft.

Celadon
A Chinese green porcelain. This was the first colour produced by the Chinese during the Sung Dynasty, A.D. 960–1276. Its delicate greenish glow was widely imitated by later Continental and English porcelain manufacturers.

Celestial sphere
A revolving globe on which are represented the constellations and other heavenly bodies. Early celestial spheres are very rare, but quite a number were made during the late 18th and 19th centuries.

Cellaret or wine cooler
For holding wine. It usually has bottle divisions lined with zinc. Cellarets were common before the sideboard had evolved into a satisfactory article of furniture. A great many were made in the first half of the 18th century. The casings of zinc were to contain and prevent the ice from melting. The outer body was usually of mahogany.

Certosina
A type of inlay using very small pieces of wood or hard stone in geometrical patterns. Italian.

Chair
A separate seat, for one person. A chair-bed was a light framework chair which could be opened out into a day-bed for resting. (See Armchair, Canapé etc.)

Chaise-longue
A French day-bed dating from the Empire period. Usually with only one end and no back to it.

Chalice
The wine-cup used in the Eucharist or Communion Service. The term sometimes loosely applied to any elaborate cup of metal on a stem.

Chamfer
An edge removed by a bevel. A groove cut in wood by a bevel.

Champlévé
A style of enamelling in which the ground is cut out to receive the enamel in powder form before firing. A strip of the metal is left between the scooped-out portions.

Chandelier
Glass chandeliers date from the 18th century. Also known as lustres. Many of them were made at the glass manufactory of Waterford in Ireland.

Channeling
A pattern formed by parallel grooves cut into woodwork.

Charger
A large flat dish, usually of pewter. Between 18 inches and 2 feet in diameter.

Chasing
The method of decorating silver or gold, using punches and a hammer. There are two distinct types of chasing—flat and repoussé. Flat or surface chasing is done from the front, giving definition to the metal but not cutting into it (which is engraving). Repoussé chasing is done by bulging out the metal from behind, then bringing out the detail by flat chasing from the front. Mounts for furniture, particularly French furniture of the 18th century, were often enriched by chasing.

Chatelaine
An ornamental chain, hung from the girdle or from a brooch, from which were suspended small objects such as scissors, keys and seals. Popular in the 18th and 19th centuries. Of gold, silver or base metal.

Chatoyancy

The cat's-eye effect seen in chrysoberyl cut *en cabochon* in the proper direction. Also seen in some quartzes. (See Asterism.)

Checker

An inlay of light and dark woods in alternate squares. Many chess tables were made in the 18th and 19th century in this way, but checker work was also used to decorate articles of furniture.

Chelsea

The factory was established at Chelsea about 1745. All kinds of objects were made under the direction of Nicholas Sprimont from 1750. The figures are particularly fine and much value is attached to the so-called Chelsea 'toys'. William Duesbury bought the factory in 1770 and transferred it to Derby in 1784. The porcelain was soft-paste and was decorated with Oriental blue-and-white themes as well as in a naturalistic way. The earliest mark was a triangle, to be followed by an anchor in an oval, sometimes picked out in red. Also a double anchor, and a gold anchor.

Cherry

A reddish wood that takes a good polish. Cherry ages well and has been much used for small articles.

Chest

The chest has rightly been called the 'ancestor of all furniture'. From it evolved tables, chairs, stools, cupboards wardrobes etc. The finest European chests date from the Italian Renaissance, and in England from Elizabethan times.

Chesterfield

A large upholstered settee. Supposedly derives its name from the 19th Earl of Chesterfield.

Chestnut

A hard white wood. Polished it is not unlike satinwood. Used for chair-making, particularly the rails and supports.

Chestnut is long-lasting and has some of the qualities of oak. In the 18th century is was quite often used as a substitute for satinwood.

Chest-on-chest
As its name implies, two chests or two sets of drawers on top of each other. It differs from the highboy (q.v.) in that the bottom chest actually forms the base. In the highboy the base is quite distinct.

Cheval glass
A large swing mirror mounted on a frame. *Cheval*—a horse, hence a support or frame. The cheval glass stands on the floor and presents the viewer with a full-length reflection. Sometimes known as a robing mirror.

Chiffonier
A small sideboard with drawers and cupboards. Also a chest of drawers with a mirror. The chiffonier was fashionable in the 18th century, and some very elegant and elaborate examples were made by the master cabinet-makers.

Chintz
A fine cotton cloth, glazed. The pattern is printed on one side. Used mostly for furniture, covers, curtains etc.

Chip carving
An early form of carving, executed by gouging out a simple pattern with the chisel. Late 16th and early 17th century furniture is quite often decorated in this manner.

Chippendale
(See Biographical List for dates.) The Chippendale style was elaborate and often ornate—claw-and-ball feet, cabriole legs decorated with masks at the knees etc. 'Chinese Chippendale' imitated the patterns and fret-like elaborations of the Chinoiserie vogue. In general, the Chippendale style is masculine, somewhat baroque, but of excellent proportions.

Chocolate pot

First made in Queen Anne's reign. Of plain silver, they were tapered and cylindrical. In Georgian times they grew considerably more ornate, with elaborate swags and floral decorations. These later chocolate pots were both engraved and chased.

Chryselephantine

Made of gold and ivory. A style of work sometimes adopted in the Italian High Renaissance period. Pheidias' famous statue of Athene in the Parthenon is the first Chryselephantine work on record.

Circassian walnut

A figured walnut used for veneers.

Cire-perdue

The lost-wax process of casting in which a wax model is invested in a fire-proof material, the wax melted out (lost) and molten gold or silver forced into the mould.

Clavichord

Father of the pianoforte. First made in the 15th century, keyed and stringed. From the Latin *clavis*, 'key', and chord.

Claw-and-ball

Introduced into England late 17th century. A characteristic of the Queen Anne and Chippendale period. Much favoured by Chippendale. The claw-and-ball foot probably originated in China.

Claw set

A method of mounting gemstones in which minute 'claws', sometimes mounted on a 'coronet', hold down the crown facets of the gemstone. One of the most secure and efficient methods of securing large and important gems.

Cleavage

The property of certain gemstones, such as diamond and topaz, to split along one or more definite directions, parallel to a possible crystal face.

Clock

Domestic clocks came into use at the end of the 16th century. Short 'bob' pendulum and minute hand introduced in the middle of 17th century. The long-case clock was first made about 1680. The earliest efficient English clock was the lantern or bird-cage (q.v.). The long-case clock reached a peak of perfection under such master horologists as Thomas Tompion and George Graham. Nearly all the great 18th-century cabinet-makers turned their attention to perfecting the case-work of long-case and mantel clocks.

Clock jack

A mechanical iron contraption for turning meat on the kitchen spit.

Cloisonné

Cell-enamelling, in which narrow strips of gold or silver wire are bent to form cells and soldered to the base, the cloisons or compartments being filled with enamel.

Close caned

Cane seats and panels in furniture, when no openings are left in the pattern. As opposed to the open, or coarse caning, of early Carolean work.

Club foot

A plain flat foot introduced about 1700. The leg tapers towards the foot which resembles an animal's hoof. Sometimes known as 'Colt's foot' and in use throughout the 18th century.

Coalport

Originally established at Caughley (q.v.) c. 1750. Transferred to Coalport, Shropshire, by John Rose in 1780. Tea services of the 'egg-shell' type were made, as well as innumerable ornaments and household articles. Much of the Coalport ware is attractively decorated with floral sprays etc., especially the late Coalport when artists like Billingsley were employed. Marks—the word Coalport, monogram C.B.D. and several other variants.

Coaster

A decanter-stand of silver or plate on wood base. The bottom is covered with baize to slide decanters along the table, introduced about 1750. Coasters are invariably circular.

Cock-beading

A narrow beading round edges of drawers etc. introduced about 1730. Cock-beading projects above the main surface.

Cocoanut cup

A cup made out of a cocoanut shell, usually mounted on a silver foot with silver rim. Early 16th-century examples are rare, but cocoanut cups were widely made on the Continent in later centuries.

Coffee pot

Coffee reached England in the mid-17th century. Silver coffee pots were introduced about 1685 and followed much the same lines as chocolate pots (q.v.). Georgian coffee pots were tall and elegant, sometimes decorated but more usually left plain. The octagonal shape became fashionable and to some extent displaced the cylindrical pot.

Coffer

An early type of chest or trunk, for keeping valuables.

Coffin stools

Usually of oak or elm. Rectangular in shape on short, strong legs, they were $1\frac{1}{2}$ to 2 feet long.

Coffre fort

A strong-box similar to a coffer in which valuables were kept. Like the later chests and coffers they were quite often elaborately decorated.

Collet set

A development of box-setting (q.v.) in which the sides of the box are filed down to expose more of the gemstone to the light.

Commode

An ornamental chest of drawers, introduced from France

into England in the 18th century. The typical commode of this period has the French Bombé shape and is often an elaborate article with chased mounts, marquetry work etc.

Composition

Somewhat similar to Carton pierre (q.v.). A mixture of whitening, resin and size. Used for the decoration of ceilings etc. Introduced by the Adam Brothers. Composition soon supplanted carved work on ceilings and walls, and was in its turn supplanted by the still cheaper carton pierre.

Concave

A surface curved like the interior of a circle or sphere. Convex is its opposite.

Concertina frame

A term used in connection with some small tables, where the rear legs open out like a concertina to support a folding flap.

Confidente

French. A settee with seats at each end outside the arms. Similar to canapé confident.

Console (Console table)

A bracket. In the console table, the bracket projects from the wall supporting the rear of the table, while the front end is supported by either one or two legs. Fashionable in the late 18th century, console tables often had marble tops and elaborate caryatid or scroll-shaped legs.

Coquillage

French—'shell-fish'. A shell pattern used to decorate frames and mirrors. This basic shell-pattern is often elaborated with amorini, swags of fruit etc.

Corbeil

French. Basket of flowers or fruit used as an ornamental motif.

Corbel

An ornamented bracket or projection.

Cordovan leather
From Cordova, the Spanish town. A type of leather, supposedly introduced into Spain by the Moors. Being both soft and durable, it was widely used in leather seats and backs for furniture.

Corner chair

A chair with a square seat, but with the seat fixed diagonally so that one corner is in front.

Corner cupboard
Made, as their name indicates, to fit in the corner of a room. They were widely made in the 18th century—from the farmhouse corner cupboard, to the elegant glass-panelled cupboard made by a London cabinet-maker.

Cornice
The horizontal, moulded projection at the top of a piece of furniture. In architecture the horizontal, moulded projection crowning a building.

Cornucopia
The Horn of Plenty. A goat's horn overflowing with fruit and flowers and corn. An ornamental vessel of this shape. Often depicted in carvings etc. as being poured out by the figure of Ceres, goddess of the Harvest. A popular motif in England during the Classical Revival of the 18th century.

Coromandel
A type of calamandar wood. A light brown with dark streaks, it comes from the East Indies. Used a great deal for small wooden articles, treen etc.

Couch
A development of the day-bed, the couch usually has supports at both ends and at the back.

Court cupboard
A cupboard with its upper story set back from the lower.

Originally it was a chest opening at front, and set on a table. Ancestor of the sideboard. Usually of oak. It was very elaborate in 17th century, but quite simple in Tudor times.

Courting glass

A mirror, possibly of Chinese origin. Set in a box, it was framed with strips of coloured or painted glass.

Crackle glass

Glass with a network of fine cracks. Of Italian origin. To produce this 'crackle' the glass is suddenly cooled while in the process of being blown.

Cradle

Early examples are of oak and heavily constructed. In woods and styles, cradles over the centuries follow the prevailing fashions of joiners, and then cabinet-makers.

Crane, Chimney

An iron bracket designed for swinging pots etc. over the fire.

Cream jug or Creamer

Introduced about 1700. Many attractive cream jugs were made in silver during the 18th century, also in Sheffield plate and porcelain.

Cream ware

A type of earthenware first made by Wedgwood from Cornwall clay. Cream ware was made from the mid-18th century onwards.

Credence or Credence table

Originally a small table used at Communion for the consecration of the bread and wine. Later a cupboard on legs, or small buffet, used in Tudor and Elizabethan times for food and drink. The credence table, like the buffet, later became an article for the display of plate.

Crenate

An edge having a notched or toothed appearance.

Creole ear-ring
A metal ear-ring in the shape of a hoop or circle, the lower half of the circle usually being thicker than the upper.

Cresting
Ornamental carving at the top of a chair back. Frequently very elaborate in the Carolean period.

Cretonne
Strong cotton cloth in imitation of French chintz. Unglazed and printed on one side.

Crewel work
Fancy silk or woolwork on linen much used in the late 17th and 18th centuries for bed-curtains, draperies etc.

Crib
A child's cot. As opposed to the cradle, usually only for sleeping, and for infants rather than older children.

Cricket
Scottish. A small, low stool.

Cricket table
Similar to a cricket. A triangular table, with three straight legs. Early and Jacobean, with triangular or round top.

Cromwellian chair
A simple 'austerity' chair of the Commonwealth period. Seat and back of leather, and undecorated wooden frame.

Cross banding
A banding of veneer placed so that the grain runs across that of the background.

Cross rail
A horizontal rail or splat connecting the uprights of a chair back.

Crown
The upper part of a cut gemstone.

Cruet
First introduced in Queen Anne's reign. It contained silver-mounted glass bottles for oil and vinegar. Later and more

elaborate cruets in the 18th and 19th centuries held silver casters, mustard pots and other glass bottles for spices and sauces.

C-scroll

Derived from its resemblance to letter C, the scroll was often used in the 18th century as an ornament on chair splats.

Culet

The small facet (sometimes omitted) at the base of a diamond. Not often found in stones cut before the 19th century, but always in modern diamonds.

Cupboard

First known as such in Tudor times. The cupboard developed out of the hinged chest and then became an article on its own.

Cupid's bow

A Neo-Classic design used at the top of chairs and employed, among others, by Thomas Chippendale.

Cup plate

19th-century pottery or glass design for those who preferred drinking tea from the saucer. Cup plates, like moustache mugs, were once very common but comparatively few now survive.

Cup turned

A turned leg with a cup-like bulge. The leg is tapering. Popular in 18th-century furniture and very common in the 19th century. Introduced into England in the 17th century.

Curule

The most common chair of antiquity. The curule was something like a camp stool with fabric or leather top, but the X-shaped legs were often elaborately decorated.

Cylinder-fall
A curved sliding top fitted to writing tables. The true cylinder-fall is a solid piece, and not of the Venetian-blind type.

Cyma curve
From Greek 'Kuma', a wave. The ogee moulding of a cornice. Anything showing a wavy curve—as in a cabriole leg or certain types of chair back.

Cypress
A fine-grain wood of great durability. Reddish colour. Cypress was often used in early days, where cedar was later used, as chest or drawer lining.

D

Damask
A fabric of cotton, linen, silk or wool with floral and other patterns produced by the weaving process. The figures and floral patterns are often in contrast to the background. Its name derives from Damascus, whence it was introduced into Europe during the 14th century.

Davenport desk
A small writing desk which became popular in the 19th century. It has a sloping top with drawers underneath. Drawers are usually fitted on one side of the desk and complementary 'blind' drawers on the other. (See Bureau.)

Davenport ware
Made at the Longport works of John Davenport, established 1793. Earthenware and porcelain were produced here, the style being somewhat similar to Derby (q.v.).

Day-bed
The ancestor of the sofa and chaise-longue. An elongated chair of oak or walnut. Usually with carved or turned stretchers and several legs. The backs were cane and the

seats were brocade covered. Like so many other pieces of furniture it was Near Eastern in origin. Introduced in the Jacobean period and very popular at the time of the Restoration.

Deal
Timber of fir and pine. Straight grained, and easy to work, deal has been used by joiners and furniture makers since Tudor period.

Decanter
A glass bottle for holding decanted wine. In use from late 17th century onwards. Early forms generally had a bulging body, but the popular square decanter appeared in the second half of the 18th century. Glass stopper to match. The neck usually ringed and stopper ornamented.

Degame wood
A West Indian hardwood. Used for decoration, it is yellow in colour.

Delft ware
A tin-glazed ware made at Delft in Holland since the early 17th century. Blue at first and later polychrome. English Delft was made principally at Bristol, Lambeth and Liverpool. The clay was coated with an opaque white enamel on which the designs were painted in various colours.

Dentil or Dentel
A tooth-shaped ornamentation. Used in furniture and woodwork and interior decoration. Small blocks alternate with equal-sized open spaces, rather like the crenellation of a castle's walls. Most commonly used for cornices.

Derby
The original pottery established about 1750. Taken over by William Duesbury in 1756. Soft-paste porcelain, table services and figures were produced. Best work done after Duesbury had bought the Chelsea works, 1770–1775, also in the Crown Derby period, 1785–1790. The modern Crown

Derby works was established in 1876. Marks—D in gold, D with an anchor. After 1773, D with a crown above it, later two cross staves were also added. A number of other later marks.

Derbyshire chair
A 17th-century type, the open back supported by cross rails. Straight uprights rising to a scrolled top.

Desk
See Bureau.

Diamanté
White paste used for imitation jewellery. This type of white 'diamond' paste is sometimes referred to as Strass (q.v.).

Diaper work
Ornamental design for panels. Flowers, leaves, geometrical patterns etc. repeated in a reticulated pattern, rather similar to the reticulated patterns found in textiles.

Dished corner
A depression near the corner of a table top to hold cards and counters. Commonly found in 18th-century card-tables, also sometimes in writing tables to hold a candlestick.

Dish-top
A table top with a raised rim or edge. Quite commonly found in circular tables of the 18th century.

Divan
Of Eastern origin. An upholstered sofa, backless.

Dole cupboard
A name commonly given to early cupboards with pierced or fretted panels, used for storing food. The original dole cupboards were designed for the dole bread given to the poor at monasteries and other religious institutions.

Dop
A holder for the diamond while it is being bruted and polished. (From an old Dutch word meaning, shell, the

shape of the brass cups originally used for holding the diamond during polishing.)

Double chair

An open-back settee for two persons. Popular in the Queen Anne period. Like the Confidente (q.v.) it was French in origin.

Doublet

A composite stone consisting of two genuine stones, or one genuine and one imitation, cemented together so as to appear to be one large genuine stone.

Doulton

A glazed stoneware produced at Vauxhall, and later at Lambeth. The works founded by John Doulton.

Dovetail

A method of fastening wood together by cutting one section like a wedge, or dovetail, so that it fits exactly into a corresponding wedge-shaped opening. Before the discovery of dovetailing, furniture had been held together by metal or wooden dowels (q.v.).

Dowel

A wooden pin used to join timbers. Sometimes also applied to iron pins. Old dowels are usually square or polygonal sided. Much used by the joiner in early furniture making.

Dower chest

A large chest usually of oak. The dower chest held the bride's dowry, clothes and personal belongings. It was consequently an important article in early days, and was often panelled and quite elaborately decorated. Drawers were sometimes fitted in later chests.

Draught chair

A winged chair designed to keep off draughts. Early draught chairs were of wood construction with only a padded seat, but later 18th-century designs were upholstered or leather-covered.

Drawer runner
The strips of wood under the drawers, on which they run. One of the tests of good cabinet-making is the ease with which the drawers will run in or out at only a light touch.

Draw table
A table with two leaves which, when pulled out, allow the table top to sink to the level of the leaves—thus doubling the size of the table. Probably first introduced during the Jacobean period and made consistently during the following centuries.

Dresden
The works were established at Dresden in 1709 and later removed to Meissen. An early porcelain was made from kaolin in 1715. The best work was produced during the so-called 'Kings Period', 1778–1796. Böttger discovered the secret of making hard porcelain either at Dresden or Meissen in 1709. Chinese styles were copied, and much of the later work had a rococo flavour. Ornamental pieces, birds, flowers and figures were produced as well as large vases, centre pieces etc. Many famous modellers and sculptors such as Kandler worked at Dresden. Marks—early, A.R. in blue ; the Staff of Mercury; from about 1726, crossed swords.

Dresser
An article of kitchen furniture, related to the cupboard. The shelves are doorless, save at the bottom. The Welsh dresser (q.v.) has become a collector's item.

Dressing table
Part of the bedroom suite, the dressing table developed from the lowboy in the middle of the 18th century. A mirror and nests of drawers, with knee-hole in middle are features of this type of table. Some of the most elegant were designed by Sheraton.

Drinking glasses
The English glass industry began towards the end of Elizabethan era. Best period between 1780 and 1810. The first glasses were introduced into England from Venice, and the early glass masters were nearly all of Italian origin. Drinking glasses are usually defined by their type of stem—plain, baluster, air-twist and cut.

Drop-front
A desk lid which, when opened, is supported on slides and forms the surface for writing.

Drop handle
A pear-shaped hanging handle. Dating from second half of 17th century. Either of iron or brass.

Drop-ornament
Any ornament depending from the under-frame of a piece of furniture.

Dropped seat
A chair seat which is carved to fit the body. It is lower in the middle and front than at the sides and back.

Drunkard's chair
An erroneous term for a large elbow chair. In the mid- and late 18th century a number of elbow chairs of these proportions were made—often, probably, for special clients. Thomas Chippendale designed some large elbow chairs of this type.

Duchesse
A dressing table with a swing looking-glass. A term also applied in the late 18th century to two easy chairs connected by a stool in the centre.

Duet stool
Victorian. A piano stool large enough to accommodate pianist and singer.

Dumb waiter

A circular two- or three-tiered pillar table.
A stand with tiers of trays from a central
stem, developed in the 18th century. Sometimes, a revolving stand for use on the dining
table.

Dutch foot

Somewhat similar to the ball foot (q.v.), except that the leg
of the piece of furniture swells out to a bulge at the foot.

Dutch style

Characterised by marquetry, walnut, bombé fronts and ball
feet. The so-called Dutch style had a profound effect on
English furniture, and it was the influence of Dutch craftsmen—brought over in the Restoration period—which led
to many major improvements in English cabinet-work.

E

Earthenware

Simple baked clay. Pottery of clay too porous for domestic
use and requiring glaze. Earthenware is the basis of all
pottery and porcelain, biscuit-coloured and fired at low
temperatures.

Ébéniste

A French-cabinet maker. Cabinet-making was a highly-
developed craft in France some time before it had become
so in England. The Paris Guild of Ébénistes was extremely
influential, and its members almost as highly regarded as
painters, sculptors etc.

Ebony

A hard, close-grained black wood used for veneering fine
furniture. Heavier than water, ebony has dark brown and
green stripes in its texture. Greatly regarded in France

during the 18th century, it was also used on many English and French pieces of furniture during the 19th century.

Egg-and-Dart

Also called Egg-and-Tongue. A design consisting of alternate egg shapes, and dart, anchor and tongue shapes. Used as a moulding on architectural ornament.

Elbow chair

A chair with elbow rests. A carver chair in a dining-room suite.

Electrum

An alloy of gold and silver composed, according to Pliny, of 1 part silver to 5 parts gold.

Elers ware

A red pottery made by the brothers Elers, who came to Staffordshire from Holland about 1690. Unglazed and ornamented in relief. Sometimes a black ware.

Elizabethan

The furniture of 1558–1603. Usually oak. Elaborately carved chests, court cupboards etc. The influence of the Italian Renaissance was predominant. Carving was ostentatious, with Classical figures and themes, bulbous baluster legs on chairs, cupboards and tables. Inlaying with cherry, holly, sycamore etc.

Elm

A hardwood with marked grain. Used for making chairs etc. Long-lasting and suitable for turning, elm has long been popular with English country chair-makers.

Embossing

A technique used in metal-work of making raised ornamental designs. They are pressed or beaten out from the back. Embossed designs will be found in articles as different from one another as copper kitchen utensils and silver brooches.

Emerald cut

The step or trap cut. Usually oblong or square, the facets are arranged in a series of steps to display the full colour of the stone, rather than to effect brilliant play of light. Called the emerald cut because of its suitability to the emerald's rich colour, but also used for other colourful gemstones.

Empire style

The furniture of 1793–1830. It derived largely from styles of ancient Rome and Egypt and became predominant in Napoleonic France. French designers such as Percier and Fontaine (later much imitated in England) helped to popularise the dignified and classical lines of this style. The furniture was often painted, and the favourite wood was mahogany.

Enamel

The art of coating metal, pottery or porcelain with fused and coloured glass. Limoges enamel—a painted enamel—is famous. (See Cloisonné, Champlévé etc.)

Encaustic

Burned-in colour. Encaustic painting was a technique in which a base of beeswax was overlaid with finely-powdered chalk. After the design had been drawn and painted upon this surface, the whole was heated and the wax 'fixed' the paints and the chalk into a durable surface.

Encrusted enamel

Enamelling on the round, applied to surfaces in high relief, and used extensively in Renaissance jewellery.

Endive

A carved scroll resembling an endive leaf. Popular during the mid-18th century.

Endive marquetry

A type of 'seaweed' marquetry of intertwined stalks. Fashionable in the William and Mary and Queen Anne periods, and most probably brought to England by Dutch craftsmen.

Engraving
A linear pattern achieved by cutting away the surface of the metal with a sharp-pointed tool called a graver. The decoration of silver or other metals by cutting in this manner. In general, the technique of decorating by incised designs. Also, the impression taken on paper off an engraved and inked copper plate.

Enseigne
A hat ornament worn by men in the 16th century, often bearing their monogram or an inscription. Usually made of gold, decorated with enamelling etc. and sometimes set with gemstones.

Entrée dish
Introduced in reign of George II. The dish and cover could

both be used as dishes, the cover having a detachable handle. Made in silver, and later in Sheffield plate. Many entrée dishes fitted into an outer cover which held hot water to keep the dish warm. At a later date the dishes were suspended over spirit lamps.

Épergne
A centrepiece for the dining table. Often extremely elaborate, with fruit bowl and dishes for sweets. The épergne became one of the great display pieces of the 18th-century dining table, and all the master silver craftsmen vied with one another in the complexity and ornateness of their work in this field.

Escallop shell
Ornament like a shell. The pattern based on the scallop shell, and very popular as an ornament for furniture and interior decoration since the 17th century.

Escritoire
An elegant French cabinet or table. Usually fitted with drawers and pigeon holes, it was (as its name suggests)

designed principally as a writing table. In the hands of the great French ébénistes it became one of the most modish and luxurious pieces of furniture.

Escutcheon
Shield-shaped ornament or shield with armorial device. A key-hole plate. These were so called because of their shield shape. Usually of brass, they were designed to accord with the door handles, finger-plates etc.

Etagère
French. Open wall-shelves or brackets. Designed for the display of *objets d'art*, porcelain etc., they were made in many styles. They are sometimes mirror-backed. The term is also applied to small drawing-room tables with several tiers.

Etruscan
Black ware of ancient Etruria. Sometimes decorated with figures, they were used as cinerary urns. The discovery of a number of them in the 18th century prompted an 'Etruscan enthusiasm' and led, among other things, to Wedgwood calling his pottery works 'Etruria'.

Ewers
Ewers were used in medieval times, and later, for washing the hands at table. They probably reached Europe from the Near East. Before the Renaissance—and the use of the knife and fork—the ewer was important for keeping the diner's hands clean.

Extinguisher
A metal cap for extinguishing candles. A normal adjunct to the old brass candlestick.

F

Facet
One of the small flat surfaces of a cut gemstone. Hence 'faceted'—a gemstone that has been cut to reveal its best properties.

Faenza
Majolica or tin-enamelled ware from Faenza in Italy. Made at the end of the 15th century, Faenza ware is perhaps the finest majolica ever made. Blue and yellow colours predominate.

Faience
French tin-enamelled ware, deriving its name from Faenza where it originated. A type of glazed porcelain or earthenware, sometimes used for beads, had been made in ancient Egypt. All modern faience stems from the Italian 15th-century majolica work.

Faldstool
A folding stool. Of ecclesiastical origin, the faldstool was used by the priest for resting during a service. The frame is X-shaped and the seat usually covered with velvet or other sumptuous material. The term is also applied to the small desk used in the Church of England during the litany.

Fan back
A type of Windsor chair, with its back spread like a fan.

Farthingale chair
Elizabethan and early Jacobean armless chairs. So called because they were designed to accommodate women wearing farthingales (hooped petticoats). The chairs had stretched legs and tall, narrow backs.

Fauteuil
A French style of armchair. Open under arms, with an upholstered back and seat.

Feather banding
A veneer patterned like feathers.

Feather edge
An engraved feather edge found along the handle of English table plate. Old English pattern.

Fede ring
Ring with a central motif of two clasped hands to symbolise troth. (Latin *fides*: trust, faith.)

Fender
A low metal guard for surround of hearth. Originally of iron, but from the 18th century mostly of brass. Many 18th-century fenders are extremely decorative and elaborate.

Ferronière
A brow ornament. (From Leonardo da Vinci's painting La Belle Ferronière.)

Festoon
A wreath or garland consisting of inter-woven flowers, scallops, leaves. Designed so as to hang in a curve.

Fiddleback
A term used in reference to certain chairs etc. with a back or central splat shaped like a fiddle. Also refers to the grain of maple and sycamore because of its use in violin manufacture.

Fiddle pattern
A pattern popular in English table plate. The handles and the stem give the appearance of a fiddle.

Figure
The natural markings on wood. The figuring of a wood is very important in good cabinet-making.

Filigree
Delicate thread-like decoration in gold or silver wire. Also applied generally in the crafts to anything delicate and light.

Fillet
A flat narrow band or moulding.

Finial
In architecture, the ornament finishing off the apex of a roof etc. In furniture, the ornament at the top.

Fire
Flashes of colour emanating from the facets of a cut gemstone. Particularly applied to diamonds.

Fire dogs
(See Andiron.)

Fire-screen
A small screen which slides up and down a pole supported on a tripod. The finest were made in the 18th century. They have taken many forms, and the screen itself has been made of needlework, wood, papier mâché etc.

Firing glasses
Short drinking glasses made to withstand rapping on tables, when toasts were being drunk. Of heavy flint glass, and made in the mid- and late 18th century. Usually plain and simple.

Flagon
A large tankard, usually with handle and lid. They have been made of many materials—gold, silver, pewter, stoneware and plate.

Flambé
A cloudy-coloured glaze in pottery where the glaze seems to spread like a flame down the sides of the object.

Flambeau
A flaming torch or taper. A motif often used in architectural decoration and by wood-carvers. Used sometimes as a finial on furniture.

Flat carving
A style of decorating early chests and chairs. There is no attempt at undercutting or carving in relief, but the background is merely cut away to leave the design as a flat surface.

Flemish foot
A foot made of two scrolls, turning in and out. Jacobean.

Flemish scroll or curve
The 'S'-shaped scroll used on pediments in Elizabethan furniture. Also popular for legs and arms in the William and Mary period.

Flint glass
Glass containing lead oxide, sometimes used for paste jewellery because of its brilliance, but rather soft and easily scratched. Most commonly used for English drinking glasses.

Fluting
A chiselled groove resembling the grooves or fluting on Classical columns. Very fashionable in furniture, bureaux and chair legs etc. in late 18th century.

Flux
The fusible surface of an enamel. Any substance mixed with metal to facilitate its fusion, as in soldering.

Foil
A thin leaf of metal placed behind a gemstone or a paste in order to heighten its brilliance or strengthen its colour.

Foliaged
Objects decorated in any way with leaf patterns and designs are referred to as 'foliaged'.

Foot (of glass)
The base upon which a glass rests. Old glasses often have 'high feet', i.e. feet rising up towards the stem. A folded foot is where the rim of the foot is folded double.

Footstool
In Elizabethan and Jacobean times, footstools were very common and were often made *en suite* with a chair. This was necessitated by the rough rush-coverings of floors. Later the footstool developed into a separate article of furniture, and in the Carolean period often became a piece of furniture in its own right.

Fork
The table fork originated in Italy during the Renaissance, and did not reach England to any appreciable extent until

the 17th century. Early forks, following the Italian pattern, were 3-pronged. The 4-pronged fork evolved during the 18th century.

Form

A long narrow bench. It was an ancestor of the chair. Like the stool, it was a general article of furniture until the 17th century, usually portable. It later developed into the settle (q.v.) with a tall back.

Four-poster bed

The four-poster bed with its hangings and drapery became a feature of English life in Elizabethan times, deriving its elaborate style and decoration from Italian forms and motifs. The most elegant and graceful were made in the 18th century. Although the four-poster continued into the 19th century, it had become almost extinct by the 20th.

French foot

A concave bracket foot. The length of the foot is invariably more than the width of the face.

French polish

During the 19th century French polish eclipsed the earlier polish or oil finish (q.v.) for furniture. Consisting principally of shellac dissolved in methylated spirit, it is given its colour by various dyes. It has a harder, more glossy appearance than the old oil polish.

French style

The influence of France on all the arts and crafts has always been important in England since the 16th century. The feminine grace and elegance of French furniture, jewellery, metal-work etc. affected English fashion trends during both 18th and 19th centuries. During the Renaissance, France served as something of a clearing-house for Italian designs and ideas, bringing them into fruition before passing them on to England.

Freshwater pearl

The product of the pearl-bearing mussel (unio margaritiferus). Found in Great Britain in the rivers Tay and Spey. Freshwater pearls have been used in English jewellery throughout the centuries, and were popular during the Victorian period.

Fretwork
Perforated woodwork in furniture. A term applied to open carving in wood. The patterns are cut with a very fine saw. The best type of fretwork is to be seen in the Chinoiserie style of Chippendale. It became popular again during the 'Japanese Vogue' in the late 19th century.

Frieze
Member of entablature coming between architrave and cornice. A horizontal band of carving filling this space. In general, any broad band of decoration.

Frog mugs
Made at Sunderland. Inside is a model of a frog which is revealed as the contents of the mug are drunk.

Fuddling cups
A group of cups joined together with an opening from one to the other. Lambeth and early Staffordshire. The cups are arranged in a triangular shape.

Fulham
Pottery from the works of John Dwight, who also produced, c. 1703, a famous brown stoneware. A patent was granted to Dwight in 1671. This salt-glazed stoneware was one of the major early achievements in the history of English ceramics. Domestic articles were made as well as statuettes and busts. One of Dwight's well-known portrait figures was his 'Prince Rupert'.

Fuming
Darkening the surface of wood, especially oak, by exposing it to the fumes of ammonia.

G

Gadroon

 An ornamental edge like inverted fluting, formed by a series of convex curves. Often used in furniture, but particularly in silverware and plate.

Gallery

A raised edge around a table, sideboard, cabinet or desk.

Gallipot

A small earthenware jar usually with handle. Used by apothecaries. Often of Delft ware.

Games table

A small table fashionable in the 18th century. The top was usually reversible, with an inlaid chess board on one side, and a backgammon board concealed underneath.

Garde du vin

A cellaret, or wine cooler for standing under a sideboard in the central niche.

Garde-robe

A wardrobe.

Garland

An interlaced floral design, usually in form of a wreath. Popular as a motif in woodwork, plasterwork etc. during the 18th century. It derives from the Classical victor's garland.

Garnish

A complete set in pewter. Usually 12 platters, 12 bowls and 12 small plates. Hence an old term for setting a table is to 'garnish' it.

Gate-legged

A table with fall leaves supported by folding legs. In the Jacobean period, oak. Tops were of various shapes. Number of legs varied from eight to twelve. In vogue from about

1650 to Queen Anne period, but still being made into the
19th century.

Gem-stick
The holder into which coloured gemstones are cemented
for polishing.

Georgian
Usually taken to cover the period from George I (1714) to
the Regency of Prince George (1811–1820). But often only
considered to cover the reign of George II (1727–1760) to
the Regency. In furniture, silverware and all the decorative
arts, the prevailing influence was Classical and aristocratic.
The baroque was to be found, but more disciplined than
during the similar period on the Continent. During the
Georgian period the great cabinet-makers and designers
were all active—Chippendale, Hepplewhite, Adam,
Sheraton etc.

Gesso
A composition of plaster-of-Paris, gypsum, used in painting
and sculpture. Used in England at beginning of 18th century. Gesso originated in Italy. It was poured into moulds
and, when set, it could be carved, gilded and painted.

Giardinetti
A type of garland ring, popular at the end of the 17th century. Usually one important central stone is surrounded by
a garland of small coloured stones.

Gilding
Method of ornamentation using gold leaf. The technique
used by most 18th-century frame- and cabinet-makers was
to burnish the gold leaf over a prepared ground of chalk
composition. The gold leaf can also be laid onto a varnished
or sized surface.

Gimmel flask
Two spouted bottles 'married' together, one used for oil
and the other for vinegar.

Gimmel ring
A ring made to divide into two hoops, associated with betrothal. (Latin *gemellus*: twin.)

Gipsy setting
A setting in which the top of the gemstone is scarcely above the level of the surrounding metal. This is sometimes engraved in a star pattern as though the rays emanated from the gemstone.

Girandole
A branched candle bracket or candlestick, usually attached to a shaped or circular wall mirror. The wall mirror together with its fittings is also referred to as a girandole.

Girandole ear-ring
A type of pendant ear-ring having three pear-shaped drops hanging from a large stone set at the top.

Girdle
The line dividing the crown or top of a faceted gemstone from the pavilion or base. Stones are usually held at the girdle by their settings.

Glass
Has been in use by man since the civilisation of the ancient Egyptians, whence the Greeks and Romans learned the craft of glass-making. During the Dark Ages glass manufacture was almost forgotten in Europe. It returned via Venice in the 13th century and the Venetians were the master glass-makers for many centuries. Ultimately Venetian craftsmen emigrated to France, England and other countries, and the craft became widespread. Queen Elizabeth I granted a Venetian, Jacopo Verzelini, a monopoly of making Venetian glass in England in 1575.

Glastonbury chairs
From Glastonbury Abbey where such chairs were reputedly used. Back and front supports are X-shaped, the upper parts extending to form part of the back and arms.

Glaze

The coating of pottery and porcelain made from glass elements. These silicate materials not only decorate the pottery but also render it impervious to water.

Glyptic

The art of carving and engraving gems.

Gobelin tapestry

Tapestry works established at Paris by Jean and Philibert Gobelin, end of 15th century. Royal manufactory from 1664 under the direction of Charles Le Brun. During the reign of Louis XIV the Gobelin works was at its best, making some of the finest tapestries in the history of the craft. Standards began to decline in the 18th century. Gobelin work differed from Beauvais (q.v.) in the way that the Gobelin designs were worked in from the back.

Gothic

Generally, the period from 12th to 16th century. Characterised by the pointed arch in architecture, elaborate ornament, and delicate tracery in wood-carving. The furniture of the period closely followed the architecture. The Gothic Style in furniture has been revived at various times, notably in the 18th century when cabinet-makers like Chippendale made designs after the Gothic, and again in the 19th century under the influence of the architect A. W. N. Pugin.

Gout stool

A stool with an adjustable top. A number have survived from the 18th century, and it has been presumed that they may have been used for resting a gouty foot.

Grain

In troy weight there are 480 grains to the ounce. A pearl grain, on the other hand, is a weight equivalent to one-quarter of a carat.

Graining

A method of painting or varnishing woodwork to simulate the colour and grain of a different wood.

Grandfather chair

A winged upholstered chair. The descendant of the winged, oak chairs made since Elizabethan period, the grandfather chair developed during the reign of Queen Anne and was made throughout the 18th century.

Grandfather clock

Colloquial term for the long-case clock. Introduced about 1680, to enclose the long pendulum then coming into use. Thirty-hour movements and one hand only in these early clocks. Cases were plain oak or walnut, but in the early 18th century were masterpieces of elaboration in mahogany and marquetry. In the second half of the 18th century cases were almost universally of mahogany. The eight-day long-case clock was perfected by Thomas Tompion. Brass dials, elaborate finials, delicate chasing and engraving, all characterised the long-case clock of the best makers in the 18th century. The grandfather clock with painted dial and simple case was made by country and provincial makers right through the 19th century.

Grandmother clock

A small and delicate type of grandfather clock. First made late 17th and early 18th century.

Granulated work

Granaglia. Work in which minute beads or granules of gold form a raised surface decoration. First used to perfection by the ancient Etruscans, and the art revived by the Italian jeweller Castellani in the 19th century. It became very popular with Victorian jewellers.

Graver

The sharp tool used by the engraver to cut into the metal.

Greek fret

Similar to the well-known 'Greek key border', it resembles

a twisting ribbon. Much used during the Neo-Classic period of the late 18th century.

Grisaille
Painting in grey monochrome, sometimes used in enamel-work. Some very fine Limoges work was done in Grisaille.

Guéridon
A carved gilt pedestal or torchère (q.v.). Fashionable during the Adam period, they were usually rather ornate.

Guilloche
An architectural ornament imitating braided ribbons. Also used on furniture.

Gumwood
An Australian wood similar in appearance to mahogany.

H

Hall-mark
The stamped mark on English silver used since beginning of 14th century. It derives its name from the Guild Hall of the Goldsmiths' Company. The hall or town mark of London is the Leopard's Head and has been in use since 1327 when the Goldsmiths' Company received its first Charter.

Handles
Furniture handles of the earliest known type in England were of wood or iron. Three basic designs predominate: the bail (q.v.), the drop and the knob. From the William and Mary period onward most handles of quality were made of brass. At a later date, matching backplates were made to accord with the handles. Chippendale, Sheraton and other major cabinet-makers and designers have left drawings of specimen handles and backplates.

Hanging cupboard
Used for hanging clothes, the hanging cupboard was the ancestor of the wardrobe.

Harewood (or Hair-wood)
A green- or yellow-stained veneer of sycamore. Popular for marquetry, especially in the late 18th century.

Harlequin table
A combined writing and dressing table. The top part folds over and encloses a writing ledge. The table has a dummy drawer-front, and a small nest of pigeon holes is designed to raise or lower itself from the table. A Sheraton design of great ingenuity and grace.

Harpsichord
A forerunner of the pianoforte. The strings are plucked by quill or leather points. Similar in shape to a small grand piano. Used in 16th to 18th centuries.

Hepplewhite style
A late 18th-century style deriving from the work and design of George Hepplewhite. (See Appendix I.) Delicate and graceful, Hepplewhite furniture uses Neo-Classical motifs —the lyre and the vase, urns and acanthus. Much use of veneering. Other favourite designs include the Anthemion and the Prince of Wales feathers.

Herringbone
An inlay design popular in the Georgian period. Imitating the backbone of a herring. First popular in late 17th century.

Hickory
Little used for furniture, being liable to damage by worms and temperature changes. Because of its tenacious qualities it was favoured for shafts, handles, gun stocks etc.

High boy
Of Dutch origin. William and Mary period. A chest of drawers mounted on another chest of drawers is technically a tallboy, but called a high boy in the U.S.A. In England a high boy is a chest of drawers mounted on a dressing table or low boy (q.v.).

Hob grate
A grate shaped like a basket. Usually of iron, but sometimes of steel.

Hock leg
A cabriole type of leg, but having a broken curve on the inner side of the 'knee'. Similar in appearance to a horse's hock.

Holly
A white wood with spotted grain used in marquetry. Holly is a hardwood and much used in veneer work. Sometimes dyed, particularly in Tunbridge Ware (q.v.).

Hood
A round arch surmounting an article of furniture particularly found in long-case or grandfather clocks of 18th and 19th centuries.

Hoof foot
A foot resembling an animal hoof. Often used in conjunction with cabriole legs. First found in William and Mary period, and later used in Adam designs.

Hoop back
A round back to a chair, as in Windsor and other country chairs.

Horseshoe table
A dining table shaped like a horseshoe. Popular in the late 18th century.

Horse trappings
Ornamental brasses used on horse harness. Of Near Eastern origin, and originally designed as charms against the Evil Eye etc. One thousand different varieties have been recorded. The Crescent was the commonest. Much copied in recent years.

Hourglass
The standard method of time measurement from the Roman period until the invention of the mechanical clock.

Hutch
Similar to a dole cupboard, ambry or almery. A chest on legs with doors, used for keeping alms. Medieval. In later periods the hutch was used for storing clothes, and was a forerunner of the chest of drawers.

I

Illusion setting
A gem setting in which the edges of the metal surrounding the stone, usually a very small diamond, are cut or shaped so that they appear to be part of the gemstone itself. They appear to enhance its size, hence the name.

Incise
To engrave or cut. Incised designs in woodwork and furniture cut with a knife or other tool. Common in early furniture, but too crude for later cabinet-makers' pieces.

Ink stand
Early stands were often of pewter, with receptacles for ink, sand and wafers used for fastening letters. Silver inkstands introduced about 1700. Later inkstands of silver and Sheffield plate were often very elegant and elaborate.

Inlay
Wood inserted in another wood to produce a pattern. Metals are also inlaid with other metals, e.g. steel with gold in the Damascene style. In furniture inlay has been one of the principal means of ornamentation. French marquetry work was among the most elaborate. (See Boulle.) Not only coloured woods but also metals, shells and ivory have been used in inlay work.

Intaglio
A carved design hollowed out of the surface of the gem. As opposed to cameo in which the background is cut away, leaving the design in relief.

Intarsia

The Italian parent of marquetry. Akin to mosaic work
except that intarsia is applied to furniture. The background
is cut away, and a design or complete picture is created out
of coloured woods, polished stones, ivory etc. Some magni-
ficent Italian work was done in *Trompe l'œil* manner, where
the objects seem three-dimensional.

In the round

In which the representation stands right away from the
background, as distinct from in relief.

Italian

Usually implying of the Italian Renaissance period. Very
elaborate decoration, mainly in walnut. Metal mounts were
extensively used, elaborate intarsia or inlay work, and many
pieces in the Italian style reveal the collaboration of wood-
worker with metal-worker and jeweller.

J

Jacobean

1603–1649. Often extended to 1688, to include the Cromwellian and Carolean period. Most of the
furniture of oak, ornamented with turning
and elaborate carving. Inlay work with
holly, sycamore etc. Strong and durable,
the furniture is beginning to foreshadow
the elaboration of later periods. Bun feet.
Gate-legged tables. Mortice and tenon,
rather than dowel, in joinery. As the period develops
walnut becomes the fashionable wood.

Japanned ware

Lacquered metal-work. Like lacquer and japanning, of
Eastern origin. It was later developed in England and at
Pontypool in Wales. An iron base was tin-plated and then
decorated with lacquers. Mid-17th century to mid-18th
century.

Japanning

Lacquer work. Introduced in Europe from the Orient towards the end of 17th century. The wood is dried (in the sun in the Orient, stoved in England) and then painted. Varnishes and gilt paints are used. (See Lacquer.)

Jardinière

An ornamental pot or jar. A piece of furniture made for holding plants. Jardinières became important features in the Victorian home during the latter half of the 19th century.

Jasper

A fine hard stoneware made by Wedgwood (q.v.). It was coloured throughout in one of the following colours: black, blue, lilac, olive, pink, sage or yellow. Decorated with relief ornaments, usually in white and in the Classical style.

Jewellers' rouge

A powdered oxide of iron hæmatite, used for the final polishing of jewellery.

Joaillerie

(See Bijouterie.)

Joiner

One who joins furniture, either with mortice and tenon, wooden dowels etc., but not with glue or metal. The joiner was the furniture maker before the elaboration of the craft introduced the new term of 'cabinet-maker' for a specialist in house furniture. The cabinet-maker, unlike the joiner, used glues, metal fastenings and screws.

Jug

A receptacle for liquids made in metals, pottery, porcelain etc. Early jugs were made in salt-glazed stoneware. Silver jugs were fashionable in the reign of George II, used for wines, beer and also for hot water (the latter with lids and canework—covered handles). Milk jugs were a late 18th century development. Many jugs were also made in pewter and plate.

K

Kaolin

A fine white clay used in making porcelain. Mixed with petuntse (q.v.). Makes the hard paste for true porcelain. Kaolin is produced by the decomposition of feldspar.

Kauri

A light yellow wood from New Zealand. Especially used for bent-wood work because of its straight grain.

Kettle front

A swelled or bombé front in furniture. Combined with swelled sides it gives a shape somewhat like a kettle.

Key-cornered

When the corners of rectangular panels are broken into squares, they are called key-cornered. A fashionable treatment of panels in the Neo-Classic style. When the corners of panels are cut off by curves or semi-circles they are known as segmental-cornered.

Kidderminster

Town in England manufacturing carpets from first half of 18th century onwards. Kidderminster carpets are two or three ply, but usually a reversible ingrained two ply.

Kidney table

A Sheraton design. Shaped like a kidney, the table usually has a kneehole and tiers of drawers.

Kingwood

A Brazilian wood similar to rosewood. Often used as bandings on satinwood veneer, kingwood has been greatly used for inlay work.

Knee

The bulging part of a cabriole leg, the knee of any leg of furniture.

Kneehole
Place to accommodate the knees. Found in writing desks, bureaux etc. from the 18th century onwards.

Knife
Table knives were used in England before forks but did not become commonly used until the Restoration, when they were made *en suite* with forks.

Knife box
Made in walnut but more often in mahogany. Usually about 1 foot high, with a sloping lid, and flat or curved front. Knife boxes became popular in the 18th century and continued in use throughout the 19th. They were almost invariably made in pairs during the late 18th century and formed part of the furniture of the sideboard.

Knife urn
Similar to the knife box but made in the shape of an urn. Usually of mahogany, they became fashionable in the second half of the 18th century during the Adam period. Extremely elegant, and made in pairs, they reflected the Neo-Classicism of the period.

Knobs
Knobs for doors and for furniture have been made mostly in brass, sometimes in porcelain. Porcelain knobs or small rounded plaques set in brass or ormolu became popular in the 19th century.

Knocker, door
Early door knockers were simple in shape and made of iron. The most elegant were made of brass in the 18th century and followed many designs. Urns and garlands were popular, also rings and dolphins.

Knurr or Knur
Hard excrescence on the trunk of a tree. Hence, a knot in wood or a wooden ball.

L

Laburnum
A fine-grained hardwood. Dark brown or dark green, laburnum was popular in the late 17th century for inlay and veneering.

Lace boxes
In the 17th and 18th centuries when lace was fashionable, small boxes, often enriched with inlay and marquetry work, were used to keep the lace handkerchiefs, cuffs and other embellishments of the dress.

Lacquer
(See also Japanning.) A resinous substance found on certain Oriental trees, and used in China and Japan to decorate wood and papier mâché etc. The lac is coloured either black, vermilion, gold, green etc. It was also decorated with ivory, lapis lazuli and jade. Lacquering was a precise and intricate art, requiring considerable skill and precision in its use. It was widely imitated in England in the 17th and 18th centuries.

Lacquered furniture
Popular in England during the periods of William and Mary, and Queen Anne. Lacquered furniture was also made, though to a lesser extent, in the 18th century. Colours used included black, red, yellow, green, buff and blue. Oriental themes and motifs were widely copied.

Ladder back
A chair-back with its cross rails one above the other like a ladder. Common in 18th century, both in country furniture and in more fashionable work.

Lamerie, Paul de
Famous silversmith. 1712–1751. Lamerie's work was in the opulent rococo style so popular on the Continent. His masterpieces included centrepieces, épergnes, candelabra

etc. His influence was considerable during his lifetime, and he is one of the few silversmiths who have given their name to a style.

Lamp stand
A small table designed to hold a lamp or candelabrum. Somewhat similar to a tea-kettle stand, but usually taller. Common in the 19th century.

Lancashire chair
One type of Lancashire chair is sometimes called a spindle back, because its back consisted of vertical spindles. Mid-18th century. The term is also applied to an earlier, Cromwellian period chair, made of oak. Tall and with a panelled back, it had a carved cresting.

Lantern clock
(See Bird-cage clock, also Clock.)

Lap
The lapidary's horizontal wheel, used for grinding and for polishing gemstones.

Larch
A tough straight-grained wood. Free from knots and resistant to wear and decay.

Laureling
Laurel leaves used as a pattern in architecture and on furniture. A classical emblem of victory, the laurel or bay leaf has been popular with designers and carvers since the 17th century.

Leather
Used for seats, backs etc. of English chairs since Elizabethan period. Cordovan leather (q.v.) was considered the best. Leather was again used by furniture makers in 19th-century work.

Leeds
Pottery made at the Leeds works of Hartley Green and Company from about 1775 to 1800. A thin cream-coloured

ware, it was distinctive for its use of pierced patterns on the rims of plates. Painted and transfer-printed. Marks: Hartley Green & Co.; A crowned G; later, LP HAWLEY.

Legs
Furniture legs are one of the most distinctive features showing changes of style and of period. In early oak furniture (Tudor period) legs were heavy and often bulbous. They were succeeded in Jacobean period by the baluster shape (q.v.). Dominant from the Queen Anne period to the mid-18th century was the cabriole leg (q.v.). Chippendale designed very elaborate cabriole legs before adopting more Oriental forms with frets. The Neo-Classic period saw the animal foot, satyr leg etc. used on many types of furniture. Very elegant were Hepplewhite's designs with tapered fluted legs in the Classical manner. The sabre leg (q.v.) became fashionable in the Regency and remained the most popular until the 1840's.

Lighthouse clock
Clock with a glass hood over the movement. Popular in the 19th century.

Lignum vitae
A West Indian wood, dark greenish-brown and very hard. Used for veneering in the 17th century, and later for small objects where durability was all-important.

Lime
A white wood, with a good grain. Easy to cut but durable, hence very popular with wood-carvers for many centuries.

Linen-fold
Popular from about 1470 to 1600. This carving pattern representing a folded napkin is reputedly derived from the folded linen over the chalice used in the Eucharist. The prevailing motif in panel-carving during Tudor period.

Linen press
A cupboard for storing linen. A large chest used for the

same purpose. Early linen presses were of oak, some later of mahogany.

Lion mask

A decoration popular for knees of cabriole legs from about 1720 to 1750. Lion masks were also used for decoration on furniture during Regency period.

Liverpool ware

A number of factories making Delft, Stoneware, Slipware etc. were in operation in Liverpool during the 18th century. The district known as Herculaneum is recorded by the mark 'Herculaneum' over a crown. Transfer-printing was in common use. Very little porcelain. The liver bird was another Liverpool mark. A Liverpool jug was a large, rounded jug with a black pattern on white body.

Livery cupboard

A Tudor and Jacobean cupboard for storing food and wine. The doors were usually pierced or railed so as to allow for ventilation.

Lock

Early locks were usually of iron; later, of brass. The spring lock was the universal type until the mid-18th century when the mortise lock was invented. Early Renaissance locks, particularly Italian, were often masterpieces of craft and ingenuity.

Long-case clock

(See Grandfather clock.)

Loo table

A circular table, often with a tip-up top. Mounted on a centre pillar with a circular base or tripod foot. Designed for the fashionable card game, Loo. This type of table was extremely popular during the 19th century and was made in considerable numbers at every level of the furniture trade.

Lopers

The slides which support the drop-fronts of bureaux.

Louis XIV

Reigned 1643–1715. The style associated with this monarch is noble and imposing. Marquetry and inlay work led to the delicate complexities of Boulle. Woods used were oak, walnut and mahogany. Ebony and lacquer work were also fashionable. Some of the greatest achievements of the French ébénistes.

Louis XV

1715 to 1774. The classical nobility of the previous period gives way to a more feminine grace and line. The rococo style.

Louis XVI

1774 to 1793. Reaction against the feminine opulence of the previous style leads to a modified Classic mode. No longer grand and imposing as in Louis XIV period, this furniture tends to be elegant and simple. In England, Sheraton's designs approximate to this French period.

Love-seat

A small upholstered settee for two persons. A small settee resembling a chair with a double back and two arms.

Low boy

A small dressing table with drawers, without a mirror. Sometimes used to support a chest of drawers when it is known as a high boy (q.v.). William and Mary period. Also found in Colonial America.

Lowestoft

Porcelain from the Lowestoft factory, established 1756–1760. Blue-and-white, Chinese patterns predominate. The factory continued in operation until 1802, manufacturing a soft-paste porcelain. Some work very similar to Worcester (q.v.). Only known mark—Crescent moon.

Lozenge

A diamond pattern popular with wood-carvers etc. in Elizabethan and Jacobean periods.

Lunate

Crescent-shaped. A favourite motif in almost all the crafts.

Lustre

The effect produced by the reflection of light from the surface of a gemstone. Most transparent stones have a vitreous lustre. Diamond is adamantine; marcasite metallic; amber resinous etc. The pendant glass drops on a candelabrum are also known as lustres.

Lustre ware

Pottery ware coated with a substance to give a metallic finish. Copper lustre is the most common, but silver, gold and purple lustres were also made. Lustre ware was first made in England in the late 18th century. Wedgwood's made lustre, as did Moore and Co. of Sunderland who specialised in purple lustre. Lustre ware was extensively produced during the 19th century.

Lyre back

A chair-back in the shape of a lyre. A feature of Sheraton designs. Extremely elegant, and often copied by chair-makers during the Victorian period.

M

Mahogany

First imported about 1710, mahogany is a West Indian and Central American hardwood. Hard mahogany used during the 18th century was sometimes called 'Spanish mahogany', most of it coming from Cuba. Mahogany is a red colour, which, after polishing, may become a reddish black. 'The Age of Mahogany' is usually taken to cover the century from 1710 to 1810.

Majolica

A pottery ware decorated with metallic lustres of tin or

lead. The best was produced in Italy in the 14th to 16th centuries, Faenza (q.v.) being one of the most famous types. Majolica is distinguished by its glowing warm enamel colours.

Malachite
A green mineral (hydrous carbonate of copper) used for ornamental purposes. It takes a high polish and in its best state is sometimes used in jewellery. Large areas of polished malachite have also been used for table tops.

Mantel
The structure above and around a fireplace. A development of the stone chimney breast, the mantel was made an important decorative feature by architects like Inigo Jones, and craftsmen like Grinling Gibbons. The Neo-Classic designs of Adam are deservedly famous.

Maple
A fine-grained white wood used in inlay and marquetry work. 'Bird's-eye' maple is obtained from the sugar maple tree. This has long been a favourite with frame-makers and inlayers for its golden colour and unusual figuring.

Marble
A type of crystalline limestone capable of taking a high polish. In the 18th century marble was extensively used in furniture for table tops, interior decoration etc.

Marcasite
The name popularly given to iron pyrites when used for jewellery. True marcasite is rare and has a different crystal structure. The marcasite used in jewellery is usually brilliant—cut on the crown, and is largely imported from France where there has long been a marcasite-cutting industry. It should not be confused with cut steel.

Marquetry
The craft of inlaying or veneering designs in coloured woods. A development of Italian intarsia (q.v.), Dutch

marquetry favoured flowers, birds etc., while English craftsmen used the 'seaweed' pattern and other formal and
abstract designs. Marquetry work became very fashionable
in the William and Mary period. (See Inlay.)

Marquise

A ring composed of a cluster of stones pointed at either end
and covering the finger as far as the joint. Marquise cut, or
navette cut, is a pointed oval.

Marrow scoop

Introduced in the reign of Queen Anne. Most scoops were
made of heavy silver and had a different-sized scoop or
trowel at each end. They were made throughout the 18th
century when bone marrow was much esteemed as a
delicacy.

Mask

A stylised version of a human or animal face. A popular
motif with carvers, silversmiths, furniture designers etc.
Particularly fashionable during the Classical Revival of the
18th century.

Mazer

A wooden bowl, generally made of maple wood, with or
without a silver rim. The mazer is an essentially medieval
design and is little found after Elizabeth I. Pewter was
sometimes used on the rim and foot. Some mazers have a
silver boss in the middle, others are mounted on a silver
foot. Possibly of German origin.

Medallion

A motif much favoured in the Neo-Classic period, consisting
of an oval, square or circular design. Originally they were
always made by the wood-carver, but in the Adam period
they were often of composition.

Millefiori

Italian—'A thousand flowers'. A Venetian technique of laying rods of many different coloured glass together to

produce elaborate designs. The technique was later used by the paperweight manufacturers of Bristol etc., but its most famous exponents were the French factories of Baccarat and Clichy.

Millegrain

A type of setting in jewellery, where minute adjacent beads of metal grip the girdle of the stone. Popular in the late 18th and 19th centuries.

Minton

Earthenware and porcelain made at the Stoke-on-Trent pottery of Thomas Minton. Established 1798. Hard and soft porcelain were made by Minton, as well as majolica and Parian ware. Marks : 'M' under two cross staves; 'M & C'; the word 'Minton' with a globe.

Minuterie

A jeweller's term for small work generally. Small pieces, such as rings and clips, produced by punching.

Mirror

Early mirrors from Classical period throughout Middle Ages were made of polished metal, silver, bronze etc. The mirror with a backing of mercury and tin amalgam was first introduced into Europe by the Venetians, and Venetian craftsmen began this manufacture in England about 1673. The mirror later developed into one of the most ornamental and important objects in 18th-century house furnishing.

Miserere

An ornamental boss or bracket on the under side of a hinged church seat. Intended to give support to a worshipper when standing, the miserere was often a small masterpiece of carving. Humorous and grotesque subjects were popular.

Mitre

An angular joint in wood moulding. First used in Elizabethan furniture, the mitre is a joint where both edges are cut at an angle of 45 degrees. The standard joint used in picture framing.

Mixed cut
A gem cut with the crown having much the same form as the brilliant. The base is step cut (q.v.) but with similar proportions to a brilliant-cut pavilion.

Mixing table
A small table used for mixing drinks in the 18th century. An adjunct to the sideboard, the mixing table was the forerunner of the cocktail cabinet.

Mohs's scale
An order of hardness for gemstones devised by the German mineralogist, Mohs. The scale runs from 1-10, with the diamond as the hardest stone at 10.

Monteith
A circular punch bowl with a detachable rim designed to hold glasses. Reputedly named after a Scotsman, monteith, who wore his coats with escalloped edges. Popular in the 17th century, the monteith became an elaborate and decorative piece of silver ware with lion's masks from which were suspended ring handles.

Moresque
Any decoration in the Moorish style. Architecture, furniture etc., both in Spain and Portugal, reflected the influence of the Moors, whose long occupation of the Peninsula left a deep impression on all the crafts.

Mortar
A vessel used in conjunction with a pestle for grinding and mincing things. Common in the house from Middle Ages until 18th century, mortars were made in wood, marble, stone and pewter.

Mortise
The hole or slot cut in a piece of wood to receive the tenon of the joint.

Mother-of-pearl
The nacreous internal layer of the oyster and certain other molluscs. Used as a form of decoration in furniture, as well as in box ware, jewellery etc. Popular as an inlay in the 17th century, and again in the 19th century.

Moulding
An ornamental edging or strip applied to, or carved on furniture. In architecture or interior decoration a moulding may be sunk below the main surface, as well as raised above it.

Mount
In furniture, metal-work like handles, ormolu fittings etc. Any metal addition, such as a silver mount to a wooden mazer or cocoanut cup.

Mule chest
A type of chest standing on a plinth which contains a nest of drawers.

Muntin
The upright section between panels.

N

Nantgarw
A fine soft-paste porcelain made at Nantgarw in Wales. The factory was founded in 1811–1812 by William Billingsley. The best work was produced during the period of Billingsley, whose fruit and flower decorations have made Nantgarw ware famous in ceramics. Nantgarw porcelain is very white and translucent. The factory closed about 1821. Marks: 'Nantgarw', or sometimes 'Nantgarw' followed by C.W.

Nef
A table ornament usually in the shape of a ship. Nefs were extremely elaborate centre pieces made of gold or silver and much in vogue during the Renaissance period. They were sometimes used, like salts, to hold salt and condiments.

Later Nefs, made during the 17th and 18th centuries, were often designed on wheels to act as wine castors.

Neo-Classic
Usually associated with the influence of the Adam brothers. The Neo-Classic style employed many of the Greco-Roman motifs found on furniture, interior decoration etc. in the pieces excavated at Herculaneum and Pompeii.

Niello
A black compound of silver, copper etc. used to fill in the engraved portions of silver and other metals. Niello work is black, thus standing out against a polished metal surface. Used on swords, box ware etc. from the Renaissance onwards, but particularly fashionable in the 16th century.

Nonsuch chests
Derives its name from Nonsuch Palace. Early Nonsuch chests were so called because they showed views of the palace, but later the term was applied to any chest elaborately carved—especially if decorated with topographical scenes.

Notching
A simple ornamentation in wood, much used during the 17th century.

Nulling
A succession of beads or bosses in wood-carving. Similar to gadrooning (q.v.), it was popular for the decoration of oak furniture in Elizabethan and Jacobean periods.

Nursing chair
A low-seated chair, often made of birch and usually with a cane-panelled seat and back.

Nutmeg grater
Very common in 18th century, when nutmeg was popular with spiced wine and mulled drinks. The grater itself was usually made of steel but was often contained in a silver case.

O

Oak

The most famous of all English woods. Durable and suitable for all kinds of joinery work, oak was the principal furniture wood until the Jacobean period. For certain types of furniture it has never been superseded. 'The Age of Oak' is usually considered to be the period between 1450 and late 17th century. Oak can be light or dark in colour. It mellows with age and polishing to a rich dark brown. Swamp or bog oak is almost black and became very popular in the mid-Victorian period.

Occasional table

A light, portable table. Originated in the 18th century and developed throughout the 19th to serve a variety of purposes, from tea-table to card- and work-table. Usually on a central pillar, although many 19th-century examples were made on the gate-legged principle.

Ogee

A moulding in furniture or architecture showing a double continuous curve. Also two curves meeting at apex.

Ogee foot

A bracket foot formed of two 'S' curves.

Oil finish

Oil finish or polish was the treatment of furniture with boiled linseed oil, followed by a last polish of beeswax and turpentine. Oil polishing required a great deal of hand polishing and many hours of careful work. It was superseded by oil and varnish polishing or French polish (q.v.).

Old English

A style of table plate very popular since the 18th century. The stems of the spoons, forks etc. are flat. The ends are rounded and turned down, or under.

Olive wood
A greenish-yellow wood. Used in veneering and marquetry, and for small articles, treen, boxware etc. Mediterranean salad bowls and their appropriate salad knives and forks are often made of olive wood.

Onion foot
An early type of furniture popular in William and Mary period, and earlier. As its name suggests, the foot is turned and resembles the vegetable in shape.

Ormolu
A type of brass with about 75 per cent copper to 25 per cent zinc. Popular with French cabinet-makers for ornamental fittings, ormolu is quite similar to gold in appearance and, was often lacquered to avoid tarnishing.

Orrery
A clockwork device for showing the movements of the planets and stars, called after the Earl of Orrery. c. 1700.

Ottoman
A backless, cushioned seat of Turkish origin. Became popular in England in the early 19th century.

Overlay
Ornamenting an article by laying some form of decoration on top of it.

Overmantel
A mirror or other structure placed over and above a mantel-piece. Overmantels became popular in the late 18th century and were very common in the Victorian period.

Oviform
In the shape of an egg. Similar—ovate and ovoid. A term applied to mouldings, vases, finials etc.

Ovolo
A convex moulding of quarter-circle or quarter-ellipse section, receding downwards.

Oxford frame
Type of frame popular in 19th century where the frame pieces project at the corners so as to form a cross. Not mitred (q.v.) like most picture frames.

Oyster shell
A veneer with a ring-like grain rather resembling an oyster shell. Made up from cross-sections of finely-grained wood. Probably Dutch, and popular in William and Mary period.

P

Pad foot
Foot that terminates or rests on a pad shape.

Padouk
An Australian hardwood. Somewhat similar to rosewood, but greyer in colour.

Pagoda top
A tower of pyramidal form, as Chinese pagoda. Often found in Chippendale period furniture made in the Chinese style.

Paillons
Small pellets of solder. Used in jewellery.

Palisander
A close-grained hardwood. (See Purple heart.)

Panel
A wood moulding in a surrounding frame. The frame may have either raised or sunken mouldings. Panelling was very popular for interior decoration in Elizabethan and Jacobean periods. (See Linen-fold.) Panels in furniture became widely used in late Jacobean period. Furniture panels are also made of marquetry, needlework etc. Decorated or painted panels became fashionable in the 18th century, one of the best-known artists engaged in this work being Angelica Kaufman.

Papal ring
The ring conferred on the Pope at his investiture. The term is also loosely applied to describe any large ecclesiastical ring.

Pap boat
A child's feeding bowl with a lip from which to drink. Quite common in the Georgian period.

Paper scroll
The scroll on the top rails of chairs. Also called an 'S' scroll or volute. This type of top rail was very popular in the 18th century.

Paperweight
Made in the 19th century both in England and France. The finest came from Baccarat and Clichy. (See Millefiori.)

Papier mâché
French in origin. A composition of pulped paper used for small work such as boxes, trays etc. Very popular during the 18th century, papier-mâché articles were decorated by some excellent artists, and in a variety of styles. The craft declined during the 19th century when mass-production cheapened and coarsened the workmanship. Sometimes inlaid with mother-of-pearl and paste gemstones. The best 18th-century work, with its use of bronze and gold powders, and its attractive topographical scenes, is deservedly sought after by collectors.

Parchemin
A carving pattern similar to rolls of parchment.

Parian ware
An unglazed ware, called after its supposed resemblance to Parian marble.

Parquetry
Flooring formed by different woods laid in patterns. Akin to a coarse form of marquetry.

Partridge wood
A Brazilian wood used in marquetry, of reddish-brown colour.

Parure
A suite of matching jewellery. The parure became fashionable in the 18th century and was extremely popular for day and evening wear in the Victorian period. The parure might be set with any gemstones, from diamonds to lesser gems such as the amethyst. Usually set in gold.

Paste
A type of glass usually containing a proportion of lead oxide, and cut to resemble gemstones. The best 'diamond' paste is sometimes called strass (q.v.).

Patera
A small round dish or base used in ornamentation. Paterae are also oval or elliptical and carved in a variety of styles. Very fashionable on furniture and in interior decoration during the late 18th century.

Patina
The colour and surface found on old furniture. Patina is one of the best guides to the age of furniture, and should be carefully preserved and not eliminated by modern french polishing. The term is also applied to the bloom or film found on old bronzes due to oxidisation.

Pavé setting
A gem setting in which the stones are placed close together, so that very little metal shows between them.

Pavilion
The lower section of a cut gemstone. The part below the girdle (q.v.).

Pear wood
A reddish wood with fine hard grain. Used in marquetry and inlaying and also for small pieces of furniture and box ware, treen etc.

Pectoral
Ornament or cross worn on the breast; also the breastplate set with gemstones worn by the Jewish High Priest.

Pedestal
Any support, but usually in furniture, the main column of a tripod table etc.

Pedestal sideboard
A sideboard, whose top is supported by fitted pedestals or cupboards at the ends.

Pediment
A decorative feature surmounting a piece of furniture. Usually of curved shape, in its earlier form it is often an unbroken scroll or arch. During the 18th century the most fashionable form was the broken arch.

Pembroke table
A table with two hinged flaps. Often used as a breakfast table in the mid-18th century. The table contains one drawer and is oval in shape when the flaps are raised.

Pendant
Hanging ornament. Also any piece of jewellery suspended from another section, e.g. pendant ear-rings, a pendant brooch etc.

Pendeloque
A pear-shaped brilliant cut.

Petuntse
One of the main constituents of porcelain, a fine white earth.

Pewter
An alloy of tin and copper. Used in the 16th and 17th centuries for domestic and ecclesiastical plate. In general domestic use until the 18th century when the pottery industry supplied public demand for household ware. The Worshipful Company of Pewterers was established in

London in 1348. Best-quality pewter has about 112 parts tin to 26 of copper. Antimony and lead were used in the coarse qualities.

Pianoforte
Developed from the harpsichord by the Italian Cristofori, about 1710.

Picture mirror
A fashionable type of 18th-century mirror which had a picture painted in the top half of the frame.

Pie-crust table
A table whose edge was carved in a scallop pattern. Developed by Chippendale into an elegant circular table with the top slightly sunk, and the scalloped edge resembling a pie-crust.

Pier-glass
A large wall mirror placed between two windows. Later, any large wall mirror. Similarly, a pier-table was originally a table placed between two windows or embrasures.

Pietra-dura
A type of Florentine mosaic work. Somewhat akin to intarsia (q.v.), but pietra-dura ('Hard Stone') work was a mosaic of coloured marbles and other suitable stones. Used largely for table tops, also sometimes on panels.

Pigeon hole
A small recess in the interior fittings of a desk, used for storing papers etc.

Pilaster
A rectangular column or part of a squared pillar. The decorative artificial pillar sometimes moulded onto a real pillar, but having no structural strength.

Pinchbeck
An alloy of copper and zinc used in imitation jewellery to simulate gold. Invented by the watchmaker Christopher

Pinchbeck, in the early 18th century. Very popular for shoe buckles, artificial jewellery, box ware and smallwork etc.

Pine
A cheap wood introduced in the 17th century to serve the place of oak in inexpensive furniture. Pitch pine is an importation from the New World and is not used in any furniture of quality.

Pineapple
The pineapple became a fashionable motif in carving during the late 18th century. Featured in a number of Adam designs.

Pipkin
A small earthenware pot or pan. Also a brass or iron coal scuttle. The pipkin, or coal scuttle, became general in the mid-18th century when coal fires superseded wood and charcoal throughout the country.

Plane
A close-grained white-wood often used in the 18th century as a substitute for beech. Many of the Hepplewhite and Sheraton style painted or gilt chairs were made of plane.

Plaque
An ornamental tablet of metal, pottery or porcelain. In furniture, a decorated disk of porcelain popular in late 18th century. Plaques on furniture were also fashionable in the pseudo-French furniture of the 19th century.

Plate
Term used to denote English articles made of silver or gold. Not to be confused with Sheffield plate (q.v.). Plates, in the sense of circular vessels from which food is eaten, have been made in pewter and silver since the Tudor period. Many silver plates were made during the 18th century. The rise of the pottery and porcelain industry spelled the end of pewter and silver, except for rare occasions, as materials for domestic plates.

Plateau
Term denoting the centre of an expanding dining table.

Plinth
Architecturally, the lower square member of a pillar or column. In furniture, the stand for clocks, bases, statues etc.

Plique-à-Jour
A method of enamelling in which the backing is removed or cut away so that the light shines through in the manner of a stained-glass window. A plique-à-jour enamel is suspended rather like a paste gemstone, being only held by a mount at the sides.

Plum
A dark yellow wood, very hard, used in inlay work and sometimes in old country-made furniture and treen (q.v.).

Plume
Feather design used in furniture and particularly chair backs.

Pole screen
A small screen, often with a needlework panel, mounted on a tall pole stand. Pole screens were made in the 18th and 19th centuries with the panel of papier mâché.

Pollard oak
The wood of oak that has been polled—i.e. cut at the top to give a bushier head. Pollarding causes a change of grain in trees. Walnut trees were also pollarded, thus altering their grain from a normal or unpollarded tree.

Polychrome
Many-coloured. Applied to pottery and porcelain, also to some Italian decoration of furniture, where elaborate paintwork was used.

Pomander
A small box or container containing perfumes. In the 16th and 17th centuries they were often extremely elaborate, made of gold or silver, enamelled, and often gem-set.

Pontil mark
The pontil is a metal rod to which glass was attached while being worked. Hence, the mark under old blown glass made by the pontil rod. After the change in glass-making techniques during the 19th century, the pontil mark is no longer found—unless the piece is a deliberate attempt at deception.

Poplar
A yellowish-grey wood used in marquetry during the 18th century.

Poppyhead
An ornamental top to the end of a church seat or pew. Either plain or carved, and commonly in the form of a fleur-de-lys.

Porcelain
A very fine kind of earthenware with a translucent body and transparent glaze. Porcelain was made in China many centuries before its manufacture in Europe during the 18th century. Usually divided into two classes—hard-paste or true porcelain, and soft-paste or artificial porcelain. Hard-paste was formed of kaolin (q.v.) and petuntse (q.v.). Resistant to great heat and most acids, hard paste was made in England at Bristol and Plymouth. Soft paste made largely from white clay and fusible glass was liable to crack when heated, but excellent for decoration. Most English porcelain is of the soft-paste variety. A third type of porcelain is English Bone China made of bone ash, china stone and china clay.

Porringer
A two-handled bowl. Designed for the hot spiced drinks popular in the 17th century, porringers were usually of silver and had matching lids to keep the contents warm.

Posset cup
(See Caudle cup.) These two-handled cups were for the old English drink of posset—a spiced mixture of wine and milk.

Post
Any corner support. Bed post etc.

Pottery
All kinds of earthenware. Opaque ware as opposed to porcelain—translucent ware.

Pouch table
A type of work-table for embroidery etc., so called because of the fabric pouch for holding silks and wools. The name would appear to derive from a design by Sheraton for a 'pouch table'.

Pouffe
A large cushion or soft upholstered couch covered in tapestry or other material. The pouffe undoubtedly derives from Ottoman furniture, but the word is French and refers to a high roll or pad of hair in coiffeur.

Pounce pot
Pounce was a very fine powder used to sprinkle on writing to dry the ink. Old inkstands of pewter and silver usually have a container for pounce, as well as a container for the wafers used to seal the envelopes.

Press
Similar to a court cupboard (q.v.). Used for storing clothes and linen, of medieval origin.

Press bed
A folding bed made to collapse into a concealing closet. Ancestor of the Victorian and 20th-century 'cupboard' or 'wardrobe' bed.

Prie-Dieu chair
A prayer chair. The seat is close to the ground and the back tall, with projections to provide a rest for the elbows. Very

common in the 19th century, used for family prayers in the home. Prie-Dieu desks have a similar shape and function.

Prince of Wales feathers
The three-plumed crest of the Prince of Wales. Three ostrich feathers surmounting a crown. A motif very popular with carvers and furniture designers during the late 18th century and the Regency period.

Punch bowl
A large bowl, similar to a monteith (q.v.). First introduced during the Restoration period and remaining in fashion until the close of the 18th century. Designed for punch, a wine or spirit drink, mixed with hot water or milk, sugar, lemons, spice etc. Early punch bowls comparatively plain and simple, later examples often elaborately chased and engraved etc. From mid-18th century onwards, punch bowls were increasingly made in pottery and porcelain.

Punch ladle
A ladle used for punch. With a long whalebone, hardwood or ebony handle, and the bowl almost invariably of silver. Coins have often been set in the centre of punch ladle bowls.

Purple heart, Amaranth or Palisander
A close-grained hardwood from British Guiana. Dark brown to dark violet in colour, with a distinct wavy grain and markings. Used for veneers and decoration.

Q

Quaich
A two-handled Scottish bowl. Originally of wood, but later of silver. From the late 16th century onwards, silver quaiches were often very decorative with their flat, pierced handles.

Quarrel
Old French for a crossbow bolt. Later, a small window in a

door suitable for the discharge of a crossbow. Later again, any small opening in a door, cabinet, bookcase etc.

Quartette tables
Nests of small tables. Lightly made, they are designed to fit within one another. A design popularised by Sheraton.

Quatrefoil
Four-cusped figure in architectural tracery. A stylised four-leafed flower contained in a circle. A four-leaved clover used in ornament.

Queen Anne
1702–1714. An important period in English furniture, when walnut was the predominate wood. Cabriole legs and claw-and-ball feet became fashionable. Marquetry and lacquer-work came into vogue, and brass ornaments on furniture. An age of well-made furniture, with a tendency towards elaboration and a Continental style of inlay and decoration.

R

Rabbeting
Step-shaped piece cut from edge of timber to fit a corresponding cut in another piece, and make a joint. To join or fix with rabbets.

Rack
A framework with rails, bars etc. for keeping articles. Pipe racks, spoon racks, letter racks etc.

Rail
A horizontal or inclined bar in furniture. A bar connecting one part of an article to another. Rails were originally structural, but later became largely decorative in chairs etc.

Rake
The angle of a chair back. Anything inclined from the perpendicular.

Rance

A cross rail connecting the legs of a chair. Also, a type of red marble with blue-and-white markings.

Rat-tail

An early pattern in English table plate, where the junction of the stem and the bowl is supported or decorated by a moulding similar to a rat's tail. Fashionable in reign of Charles I and used by manufacturers almost ever since.

Reading stand

Similar to the aquila (q.v.) or lectern of the Church in origin, but designed for use in private libraries. Most fashionable during 18th century and also made during 19th century.

Reeding or Reeded

Relief fluting, where the surface is raised in thin ridges corresponding to fluting.

Refectory table

From the room used in monasteries for taking meals. A long narrow table with several legs, stretchers near or on the ground. Generally applied to any long table, but true refectory tables invariably of oak. In common use in the Great Hall or dining room until the Jacobean period.

Reflex mirrors

Hinged mirrors fitted to the sides of dressing tables or dressing chests. Fashionable from Regency onwards.

Regency style

The style of furniture etc. during the Regency of George, Prince of Wales, 1811–1820. In general terms, the Regency period is often taken to cover the years 1800–1830. It marks a change from the Neo-Classicism of the Adam period to a Grecian or Empire style. Furniture becomes more contrived and mass-production begins to offset general styling. Egyptian themes, as well as motifs culled from Pompeii. Much influenced by Napoleonic architects and designers.

Renaissance

The revival of Classical learning and skills in the arts and crafts. Mid-15th to mid-17th century. Characterised in furniture by the use of elaborate carving, pillars and decorations. In metal-work, silver, jewellery etc. the Renaissance period is distinguished by a freedom from the restraint of Medieval Christianity, and by a new awareness in techniques, use of materials etc. Opulent and somewhat over-elaborate, the Renaissance mood in England is to be seen in the interior decoration, woodwork, metal-work etc. from Henry VIII to early Jacobean period.

Repoussé

A decoration on silver or gold achieved by pushing out the metal into relief from behind. An elaborate style of embossed ornamentation popular at various times from 16th century to late 17th century. In coarser metals such as brass etc. usually taken to mean an embossed decoration formed by hammering at the metal from the back.

Restoration chair

Typical of the Restoration period of Charles II. Cane panelled with a high back on turned legs, and often with a carved top rail embodying leaf decoration, amorini etc.

Rhinestone

A modern misnomer for paste (particularly white paste) jewellery. Properly rock crystal.

Ribband back

A chair-back carved in ribbon pattern. Popular in the mid- and late 18th century. Ribband backs are among Chippendale's work.

Riesener work

An elaborate type of marquetry work introduced by Jean Henri Riesener (1734–1806). Fashionable in Louis XV and Louis XVI period. Musical instruments, flowers and other objects are represented in bold and graceful outline. Riesener's bureaux were deservedly famous, and his chiselled bronzes are as excellent as his marquetry. One of the greatest cabinet-makers of all time.

Rivière
A necklace made of a row of graduated single stones. Usually diamonds, but rivières of colourful stones such as amethysts were also fashionable in the 19th century.

Robing mirror
A full-length mural mirror, or fixed to the door of wardrobes, etc.

Rocking chair
Reputedly of American origin. A descendant of the Windsor chair, and of 19th-century development.

Rococo
A style of decoration developed in France during the Louis XV period. Resembling rock and shell work, rococo is ornate and asymmetrical. More feminine than baroque (q.v.). Rococo style was largely formed by artists, and then adopted by cabinet-makers. Chippendale incorporated a number of French rococo themes in his designs.

Romayne work
Term for medallions showing heads in the Classical or 'Roman' style. Derived from motifs and medallions of Italian Renaissance, and fashionable in England during the late Tudor–Elizabethan period.

Rose cut
A flat-based cut covered with triangular facets, usually twenty-four in number. The most popular form of diamond cut until the discovery of the brilliant cut (q.v.).

Rosette
A decoration in stylised rose form. Very popular with woodcarvers from the Renaissance period onwards. Also a type

of glass ornament on screws used in 19th century for securing mirrors, pictures etc.

Rosewood

A fragrant hardwood imported from India. Somewhat similar to mahogany in appearance, but brittle and difficult to carve. Very popular during the first half of the 19th century.

Roundabout chair

A low-backed elbow chair of circular shape. Popular in the 19th century.

Roundel

A small disc. A decorative medallion. In furniture, a round or oval-shaped medallion or small panel.

Roundel

Glass. A bull's-eye glass in early windows.

Rout stool

Regency term. From 'Rout': an assembly or company of revellers. A long narrow stool, often with cane panels, designed for guests at ballrooms etc.

Rudd's table

A patent type of table with numerous divisions, fittings, mirrors and a slide top. Designs for it from Hepplewhite and others, popular during Regency period.

Rug

A floor covering with a thick or shaggy pile. Introduced during Elizabethan period in place of the rushes which had previously covered floors. Probably of Near Eastern origin, although the word is Scandinavian.

Runner

Piece of wood on either side under drawers to support its movement. Another name for lopers (q.v.) on which dropfronts are supported. Also a piece of wood connecting legs of tables and chairs at the bottom, and serving for structural strength.

Rushbottom

A chair seat made from rushes. Found on country furniture in early periods. Used in place of cane in country furniture for seats up to 20th century.

S

'S' scroll

An arm support and decoration of 'S' shape, popular in Carolean and William and Mary furniture. 'S' scrolls have been used by interior decorators and furniture designers as a favoured motif for several centuries.

 Sabre leg

Type of chair leg very popular in the Regency period and resembling the curve of a sabre. The most common type of dining-chair leg from 1810 to the 1840s. Sometimes carved, but usually plain in dining chairs.

Sad ware

Dull or neutral tinted, hence often applied to flat articles of pewter.

Salt-cellar

The earliest of condiment receptacles. Gold, silver or pewter. Antique salts were the principal decoration of the dinner table and marked the division between the important guests and others—hence 'Above' or 'Below' the salt. One of the most famous of all salt-cellars is by Benvenuto Cellini, in gold, and in the Vienna Museum. English salts were often Gothic steeple shaped until 17th century when they became elaborate in the Renaissance manner. Trencher salts had a depression in them to hold the salt. Salts grew much smaller and more elegant as table services developed, and as salt lost its semi-mystical qualities and became no more than an important condiment.

Saltire

A St. Andrew's cross. In furniture, the stretchers of tables and chairs which cross at centre. Also called X-stretchers. Derived from Italian Renaissance furniture and developed in England during Carolean and William and Mary period.

Salver

Tray of gold, silver, plate, used for carrying refreshments, letters, visiting cards etc. Early salvers of William and Mary period were plain with simple moulded edges. During Georgian period salvers became elaborate with engraved crests, scalloped edges, gadrooning etc.

Sandalwood

A fine-grained yellow wood used in marquetry. Like cedar, sandalwood has a fragrance which acts as a deterrent to moths and insects. Used in box ware etc., and paticularly popular in Victorian period.

Satin walnut

A light-brown wood, sometimes with black markings. Imported from America and not found in antique furniture.

Satinwood

A close-grained, yellow-coloured wood popular in Sheraton and Adam periods. Imported from West Indies and Africa.

Satyr

A stylised form of the Grecian woodland deities used in masks as ornamentation. Often found in Classical Revival of 18th century as well as in Renaissance work.

Sauce boat

Sauce boats for gravy etc. came into fashion in the first quarter of the 18th century. Early sauce boats were comparatively plain silver of oval shape. In later Georgian period they became elaborately chased and engraved, and early oval foot gave place to a trifid base.

Scagliola

A composition resembling marble. Much used in 18th

century. The composition made of glue, earth colours and pieces of marble was particularly popular for table tops. Several pier tables by Adam had scagliola tops. Black and gold were also added to the initial basic colours.

Scallop

A shell-edge design, derived from the scallop, mollusc shell. Found in woodwork, interior decoration, silverware etc. Fashionable 17th century onwards.

Scarab

A gem cut in the form of a beetle, which was worshipped by the ancient Egyptians. Often a design in intaglio was cut on the underside. The scarab was also used as a decorative motif after the 'Egyptian vogue' of the early 19th century.

Sconce

A candlestick with a handle. A wall bracket candlestick of early type.

Screen

Designed to protect from draughts or secure privacy, the screen has been important in English furniture since Elizabethan times. Fire screens of many types were made and in various materials, ranging from needlework and carved wood to papier mâché. The most elegant pole screens belong to the Chippendale period.

Screw

Used in English cabinet-making since the period of William and Mary. All early English screws were of iron or brass and flat-pointed. The modern sharp-pointed screw dates from the mid-19th century.

Scroll

Ornamental design similar to a rolled or partly rolled piece of paper. Usually when viewed in section or edgewise.

Scroll foot

A Jacobean type of foot also known as Flemish foot (q.v.).

Scrutoire
An early form of escritoire or bureau.

Seat rails
The struts below the seat of a chair. The base on which the seat is constructed.

Seaweed marquetry
Popular in the William and Mary and Queen Anne period. Intertwined stalks in graceful patterns, usually in panels. Sometimes called endive marquetry. Seaweed marquetry, although deriving in technique from the Dutch, was a particularly English style of work.

Secretary
Secretaire or escritoire. Desk or bureau, but particularly a bureau surmounted by a bookcase as first introduced in the period of William and Mary.

Sedan chair
Enclosed chair for transporting a person, carried on projecting poles. Fashionable in the 18th century, sedan chairs often have beautiful panels, as well as lacquer and inlay work. London, Brighton and Bath were the principal homes of the sedan chair.

Seed pearl
A small round pearl weighing less than a quarter of a grain.

Seignorial chair
A state chair. Usually applied to early chairs, Gothic or Renaissance, designed for important dignitaries. High backed and elaborately carved, they were sometimes surmounted by a canopy.

Serpentine front
A piece of furniture with a snake-like curve. Any article of furniture with a front which curves in and out. Very fashionable in 18th-century France, and later widely imitated in England.

Settee
A long seat with back and arms. Later examples are upholstered. Introduced in Carolean period. Derived from two chair-backs coupled together.

Settle
An antique type of bench with back and arms. In Eliza-

bethan period, often an oak chest with a back, but in Jacobean period more elaborate, and often ornately carved. Almost always of oak, and often with a box seat, the settle later became a provincial or country piece of furniture and was not made by the cabinet-makers of London.

Sevigné
A bodice ornament, often lavishly set with stones, in gold or silver. (After Mme de Sevigné, the French letter-writer.)

Sèvres
Porcelain made at Sèvres in France from 1753 onwards. Soft porcelain was made until 1769 when the Sèvres works began to produce hard porcelain. In general, Sèvres porcelain was pure white, decorated with floral designs, and made use of gilt, ormolu and blue colours. Marks: Double interlaced 'L' with the word Sèvres. Sèvres was one of the few factories to use a date letter for its pieces—thus, A 1753, Z 1777 etc.

Shagreen
A leather prepared from horse, camel and shark skin. The best is a green sharkskin. This was popular in the 18th century for decorative purposes. Used very largely in box ware and other small work.

Shank
The hoop of a ring.

Shaving table

An 18th-century device, a small table containing a basin and looking-glass. Fitted with drawers, the shaving table became quite an elaborate article during the Regency period.

Sheffield plate

Discovered by Thomas Boulsover, 1742. A method of fusing copper with strip silver so that the manufactured article was practically indistinguishable from silver. Not to be confused with electro-plating, discovered in the 19th century, and a purely industrial process, without any of the craftsmanship involved in the manufacture of true Sheffield plate.

Shell

The shell motif became fashionable in England deriving from the rococo style of France. Oyster and scallop shells were widely used by cabinet-makers, carvers and interior decorators during the 18th century.

Sheraton

(See Appendix I.) The Sheraton style depends largely upon straight lines. Legs of chairs etc. are tapered or fluted in the Classical manner, rather than cabriole (q.v.). Satinwood is popular as an inlay. Grecian or Neo-Classic motifs such as the urn and the laurel leaf are fashionable. More feminine than the Chippendale style, and with a greater use of light-coloured or painted woods.

Sheveret

A type of writing table made by Hepplewhite. A number of open bookshelves rest on the top. The front opens outward to give more width, and rests on 'pull-out' legs.

Shield back

A chair-back in the shape of a stylised shield. Very fashionable in the 'Hepplewhite School'.

Shoe

The projection at the back of a seat rail of a chair designed to receive the bottom of the splat. Also the disk under the foot of a chair to prevent it damaging the carpet.

Sideboard

Derived from the table, the sideboard became an elaborate and individual piece of furniture during the 18th century. The Adam brothers gave it an architectural quality by supporting it on cupboard-pedestals. Thomas Shearer made it a graceful and specific article of furniture. Sheraton and Hepplewhite made the sideboard a decorative and elegant object—far removed from its simple ancestry.

Sideboard table

A link between the table and the late 18th-century sideboard. Sideboard tables had drawers for cutlery etc. and were often supplied with marble or scagliola (q.v.) tops.

Side chairs

As opposed to carver chairs (q.v.) or armchairs, side chairs were single chairs for the dining or drawing rooms. Uncommon in early days when the less important members of the company sat on stools or benches—side chairs became part of the normal suite of chair furniture in the 18th and 19th centuries.

Side table

Designed for setting against a wall, it became popular at the beginning of the 18th century. Its place as an article of furniture was later taken over by the sideboard. In the interim, under the hands of designers like William Kent, it had become an ornate and baroque piece often being identified with the pier table (q.v.).

Skirt

(See Apron.) The strip of wood beneath the front of the seat of a chair. Usually decorative and designed to conceal the construction.

Sleigh bed

Early 19th-century bed. Empire style. Postless, and with

foot and head boards designed to arch over in the manner of a sleigh's runners.

Smallwork
Small objects of vertu, such as cigarette-cases, snuff boxes, parasol handles etc.

Smalto roggio
A rich red enamel. Found in Italian Renaissance jewellery and smallwork, and later copied in England and France.

Snake foot
A foot found quite often in 19th-century furniture, usually on a small table or stand, shaped like a snake's head.

Snake wood
A Brazilian or British Guinean wood of red-brown colour. Very heavy, and regularly marked rather like a snakeskin, it has been used on high-quality inlay work. Rare.

Snuff bottle
A small Chinese bottle used to contain snuff or medicine. Miniature spoons are often attached to the stoppers. Fine examples made in China during 2nd half of the 18th century. Snuff bottles were made in many shapes and materials —porcelain, jade etc.

Snuffers
Designed for extinguishing candles. Similar to scissors, with a miniature box on the longer blade to catch the wick. Often with a stand or tray to match, they were generally used from late 17th century and throughout 18th century. Made of silver and Sheffield plate.

Sofa
Somewhat similar to an ottoman (q.v.). An upholstered settee, appearing early in the 18th century. A descendant of the old day-bed, the sofa usually had only one end. Late 17th century and 18th century sofas usually had a back.

Spade foot
A four-sided, tapering foot, found on chairs, cabinets etc.,
similar to a spade in shape. Popular in the second half of the
18th century.

Spandrel
An ornament for the corners of clock faces. The best brass
or gilt spandrels were hand chased and engraved—often
Classical motifs such as cherubs' heads. Found mostly on
the better long-case or grandfather clocks, but also on good-
quality bracket clocks. Clocks by such masters as Thomas
Tompion have spandrels as delicate as jewellery. Plain cast
spandrels are found on simple good clocks, and painted
spandrels on the painted dials of comparatively cheap
clocks. Also, a space between the shoulder of an arch,
moulding or framework.

Spanish foot
A grooved foot shaped rather like a hoof. 17th
century. Fashionable on the Continent, but rarely
found in England.

Spanish style
Usually associated with the use of leather for seats etc.,
elaboration in carving, and complex inlay work similar to
intarsia (q.v.). Somewhat heavy and simple in its overall
design.

Spindle
A fine rod or baluster. Often used in furniture, chair-back
etc., and deriving from the working spindle in shape. A
term applied to the spindle-shaped backs of Windsor
chairs.

Spinet
A small wing-shaped harpsichord. A successor of the virginal. One string to each note. Late 15th century. The
strings were plucked by pointed quills.

Spinning chair
Type of simple chair or stool designed for use with the

spinning wheel. The back is tall and narrow, and the construction of the chair simple but strong.

Spinning wheel

Dates from early 16th century in Germany, whence it reached England. Cotton, flax or wool were spun into threads on the spinning wheel. It became increasingly elaborate over 17th and 18th centuries, late fashionable examples being akin to cabinet-makers' work.

Spiral turning

Turned lathe work in the form of a twist. Sometimes called 'barley sugar' twist turning, especially in Carolean period when it was most popular.

Splat

The centre section of a chair-back between the top rail and the seat. First distinguished as an ornamental section in William and Mary period. Reached its peak of elaboration under the influence of Chippendale.

Spode

First produced at the Stoke-on-Trent factory established by Josiah Spode in 1770. Josiah Spode Jr. made the first type of English bone china. Spode ware was distinctive for its willow pattern, and for its floral and Japanese designs in table ware. Marks: Usually the word 'Spode'; after 1833, Copeland with two interlaced 'C's'.

Spool turning

A type of turning in the form of a succession of spools. Very popular in certain types of country chairs from the 17th century.

Spoon

Much earlier in domestic use than knife or fork. English examples date from Middle Ages. Early spoons often of wood or horn, but silver became the principal material from the 17th century onwards. Apostle spoons (q.v.) were popular in the 16th century. After the mid-17th century the rat-tail ornamentation under the bowl became popular. Later the bowl of the spoon became more pointed and the handle and bowl became of the modern shape.

Spoon back

A type of chair-back shaped like a spoon for comfort. Queen Anne period. Tended to disappear as soon as upholstered backs became general.

Springs

Coil metal springs for chairs etc. were introduced in the middle of the 18th century. At first they were largely used for 'exercise' or 'hobby-horse' chairs. In the 19th century when they were manufactured cheaply, they soon altered the whole conception of the chair-maker's craft.

Squab

A stuffed cushion. A chair cushion that fits into a grooved place in the seat and can be removed.

Standing cup

An ornate drinking cup with a cover. During the Renaissance period, these standing cups were among the most elaborate examples of the goldsmith's and silversmith's craft.

Standish

An early form of the inkstand. A stand containing ink, a holder for pounce, a wafer tray etc.

Stencilling

The decoration of furniture by stencil. Stencilling was used for borders and patterns in interior decoration for many centuries, but was not applied to furniture until the 19th century.

Step cut

(See Emerald cut.)

Sterling

Of standard value or purity. Sterling standard requires no less than 925 parts of silver in every 1,000. Indicated on London-made silver by the Lion Passant since 1544.

Stile
The vertical piece in frame of a panelled door. The upright of a frame or panel in furniture.

Stitched-up
Upholstery which completely covers chair or sofa seat to the lower edge of the frame.

Stoneware
Opaque pottery, salt-glazed. Popular in the 15th and 16th centuries. Stoneware jugs and tankards were much favoured in England, often with silver or metal lids and mounts.

Stool
The earliest form of seat in English furniture. All early stools were joiners' work, being tied with dowels or mortise and tenon joints. Later in the 18th century the stool of mahogany became a cabinet-maker's piece, often very elaborate and decorative.

Storr, Paul
A silver craftsman of great ability. He worked from 1792 until 1821. Like Paul de Lamerie, he is one of the few silversmiths who has given his name to a whole type of design. Storr's work was highly elaborate and intricate with considerable use of engraving, chasing, saw-piercing etc.

Strapwork
A type of carved ornament consisting of narrow bands interlaced in various patterns. Originally used in Elizabethan and Jacobean periods by wood-carvers for panels etc., and during 18th century by designers like Chippendale for splats of chairs.

Strass
A lead glass used for diamond imitations. Called after the 18th-century jeweller, Josef Strass.

Straw marquetry
Decoration with applied and dyed straw. Oriental in origin

and much favoured on the Continent during the 18th century.

Stretcher

The under-rails or bracing pieces of wood between legs of chair, table, cabinet. Originally intended to keep the feet off rush-covered floors, as well as to tie the furniture together. Later revived as pure decoration by designers like Hepplewhite.

Stringing

Thin fine lines of inlay, usually of contrasting colour to background wood in cabinet-work.

Studs

Large-headed nails used for decorating furniture. Brass, copper, or gilt studs were used for securing leather and other coverings to the frames of chairs, sofas etc.

Stuff over

A method of upholstering chairs. The covering material is pulled over the edges of the seat rails and is made fast out of sight along the bottom edges.

Stump bed

A bedstead without posts. A bed with headboard only. Stump beds have no footboard at the bottom.

Suite

A matching set of jewellery. Similarly, a set of chairs etc. made to match.

Sutherland table

A variant on the Pembroke table (q.v.). A type of small table whose top is so narrow, when the side-flaps are down, that it occupies practically no space.

Swag

A festoon of flowers, foliage or fruit. Used as decoration in all the crafts from carving to metalwork and jewellery. Very fashionable on furniture and plaster work in Adam period.

Swan neck
A curved design made fashionable by Chippendale, consisting of two opposed curves which meet and conclude in a scroll.

Swansea
Porcelain factory established about 1814, and famous for the work of William Billingsley. A white soft-paste porcelain was made, often decorated with flowers, butterflies, fruit etc. Marks: Crossed tridents; single trident; 'D' inside a scroll; Dillwyn & Co.

Swell front
A bow front in furniture. Somewhat similar to bombé (q.v.).

Sycamore
A type of maple. Light-yellowish colour, and often with a fine 'fiddleback' grain. A hard, even-grained wood, it has been much used for veneering. Sycamore is sometimes stained to a greyish colour when used as a veneer.

Synthetic stones
Manufactured stones having the same composition, crystal structure and other properties as the natural mineral they represent, e.g. synthetic rubies.

T

Table
Essentially an article of furniture with a flat top of wood, marble etc. Ancestor of all tables most probably the trestle table: a flat board supported on movable trestles. One of the earliest forms in England, the refectory table. Usually of oak, Tudor, Elizabethan and Jacobean tables had heavy legs of baluster shape. Gate-legged table (q.v.) Jacobean period. Pembroke tables with flaps, card-tables, tea-tables, and almost every variant produced during the 18th century to accord with the demands of fashionable life. Extending dining tables and other drop-leaf types became popular in the 19th century.

Table (jewellery)
The top flat facet of a diamond or other gemstone. Considerably larger in the 20th century brilliant cut than in Victorian and earlier brilliants.

Table chair
An early type of chair which forms a table when the back is lowered over the arms. Sometimes called a monk's seat or bench. Almost invariably of oak. Early examples very rare but sometimes made in 19th century.

Tabouret
A drum-shaped stool. An upholstered stool, or sometimes an Oriental coffee stool.

Tallboy
A tall chest of drawers. Basically, a chest-on-chest. Tallboys came into wide use during the 18th century, and the design was kept unchanged throughout the Victorian era.

Tall-case clock
A long-case or grandfather clock (q.v.).

Tambour front
A roll-top to a desk made from thin strips of wood glued on to canvas. Somewhat similar to a Venetian blind, and first used as a desk top in the late 18th century.

Tankard
A large drinking vessel of silver or pewter. Usually with a

cover and handle. Most 17th-century tankards had flat lids and were undecorated. The domed lid dates from the Queen Anne period. In the early 18th-century tankard bodies tended to be bellied or bulbous, rather than straight.

Tapestry
A picture executed by weaving. The oldest form is known as high-warp, where the warp threads were strung vertically on the loom and the craftsman interweaved the coloured

weft threads to build up the picture. The late 15th and the first half of the 16th centuries was the great age of high-warp tapestry. Low-warp looms were introduced into France about 1600, and tapestry began to be made in England at Mortlake in the early 17th century. Aubusson, Beauvais and Gobelin are three of the great names associated with tapestry. The art of tapestry-making reached Europe from the East in the 14th century.

Tapestry furniture

Tapestry as a covering for furniture was made in France in the 15th and 16th centuries. It became fashionable in England in the late 17th and 18th centuries, reaching this country from France. Furniture tapestries of the best quality are a combination of wool and silk threads, hand executed. Modern tapestries are machine made.

Tazza

Saucer-shaped cup mounted on a foot, somewhat similar to a champagne glass. Introduced from Italy in the second half of the 16th century. The tazza usually has a baluster stem and a circular foot.

Tea caddy

Originally called a tea chest. Introduced in Queen Anne's reign. Made in fine woods with inlay work. Of various shapes, but often octagonal. Usually two compartments lined with pewter, one for green and the other for black tea. In the 18th century and after often made of silver and delicately decorated.

Teak

A heavy, dark-brown Indian wood. Used in the 18th century for making furniture, but primarily used in ship-building.

Tea kettle

Tea kettles were introduced in the early 18th century. They were designed on stands with spirit lamps underneath.

Early examples are usually plain, but later tea kettles were often elaborately chased and engraved.

Tea pot

Of silver, or sometimes pewter, originated in England in the Queen Anne period. Early Georgian tea pots were usually round, small and plain—sometimes known as 'bullet shape'. Later they became oval-shaped or even angular, resting upon feet. Delicate engraving on later 18th-century tea pots. Pottery and porcelain tea pots made by all the more important ceramic manufacturers.

Tea poy

A small table usually circular, with a hinged top over a receptacle to contain tea caddies. Generally mounted on a central pillar with three legs. 18th century.

Tea table

A tripod table. 18th century. Usually with a round top and sometimes with pie crust edge.

Tea urn

A descendant of the tea kettle, the tea urn came into fashion in the late 18th century. Usually urn- or vase-shaped, with lifting handles and kept hot either by a heated iron inside or a spirit lamp. Often fluted or decorated in the Adam Neo-Classic manner.

Tenon

The end of a piece of wood cut so as to fit into a mortise for making a joint.

Terminals

Terminal ends or the extreme points of a piece of furniture. Usually decorative and fulfilling much the same ornamental object as finials.

Tester

The canopy frame over a four-poster bed. A half-tester, popular in the 19th century, extends over half the bed only.

Throwing
In pottery, to shape on a wheel. Similarly in furniture the term is applied to wood-turning. Elizabethan or Jacobean chairs with considerable turned work are sometimes referred to as 'thrown chairs'.

Thuya
A golden-brown wood figured with small 'birds'-eyes' in a circle. Used in inlay work.

Tier
The under-shelf of a table or cabinet etc. One of several shelves placed one above another.

Tiger jug
A stoneware jug, salt-glazed, of Germanic origin. Often with pewter or silver.

Toby jug
An earthenware ale jug, probably made first by Ralph Wood in the mid-18th century. Highly-coloured and representing a fat comic figure, they have been widely copied in recent years.

Toilet mirror
A small mirror supported by two uprights, with drawers for toilet requisites below. Toilet mirrors became popular in the 18th century.

Top rail
The top rail of a chair-back, often elaborately carved and crested in 18th-century mahogany furniture.

Torchère
A tall candle stand. Similar to vase stands, but often fitted with candle holders.

Tortoiseshell
More accurately turtle-shell. The mottled outer shell of certain sea-turtles used in decorative work. As a veneer for furniture, tortoiseshell was extensively used in boullework (q.v.).

Towel horse
A wooden frame for hanging towels etc. to dry. Mid-18th century onwards.

Trap cut
(See Emerald cut.)

Tray
Flat shallow vessel of wood or metal for carrying small articles. Would appear to have been introduced into England in the 18th century along with tea-drinking. Trays were lacquered and japanned, made of silver, Sheffield plate and papier mâché. The best papier-mâché trays of the late 18th century are very delicately painted and ornamented. Silver trays predominate in the latter part of the 18th century, early ones being plain and simple, later examples elaborately engraved and decorated.

Treen ware
From 'Tree'. Early English tableware, boxes etc. made generally of sycamore wood.

Trellis
A lattice or grating of light wooden cross-bars. During the 18th century trellis-work of brass was often used on bookcase doors in place of glass.

Trencher
Early plate made of wood. Later examples of pewter. Originally for serving bread, and surviving into modern times in the bread board.

Trestle
Supporting structure for a simple table or flat form. Early trestles were no more than single uprights resting on crosspieces on the floor. Medieval and early tables were almost invariably supported on trestles.

Triplet
Composite stone with crown and base of genuine material, but with an intermediate layer, usually of glass, sandwiched between them.

Tripod
Three-footed support, most fashionable in the 18th century. Almost invariably with a central pillar or column.

Truckle bed
A small low bed which can be pushed under a larger bed. Castors were added in the 18th century.

Tudor
1485–1558. A period of oak furniture during which the Italian Renaissance influence became marked in England. Architectural in conception, the furniture was often elaborately carved. Legs of tables etc. tended to be baluster or bulbous. Linen-fold panelling. Gothic forms gave way before Italianate elaboration and Classical motifs, amorini, swags of fruit and flowers etc.

Tulip wood
A West Indian hardwood of light yellowish colour with pink strips. Used in marquetry.

Tumbler
A flat-bottomed stemless drinking glass. Introduced in late 17th century, it was originally of heavy flint glass and with a rounded bottom so that it could not be knocked over but would always 'tumble' upright.

Tunbridge ware
A veneer cut from the ends of small rods of various coloured woods. Made at Tunbridge Wells and very popular for small decorated objects, boxes etc.

Turnbuckle
In furniture, a catch turning on a central screw. Also a device for connecting together two metal rods.

Turned chairs
Chairs whose legs, uprights, back etc. consist of turned work.

Turnings
Lathe-turned wood.

Turnip foot
A ball or bun foot cut off flat where it rests on the ground, similar to a half section of a turnip.

Twist
A type of spiral turning popular in furniture during the late 17th and early 18th centuries. Also called 'Barley twist'.

U

Under brace
(See Stretcher.)

Upholder
Old word for an upholdster. An upholsterer, a craftsman engaged in making upholstery fittings.

Upholstery
The covering, padding and stuffing of furniture. Originally confined to beds, but padded seats and upholstery began to be used in the Jacobean period. Upholstery was, like so many improvements in furniture and the crafts, brought into Europe from the East. 18th-century furniture was well upholstered and comfortable. The coil spring for furniture was invented in the 18th century but not in general use until the 19th.

Urn
In furniture terms, a large wooden vessel resembling a Classical urn. Usually in conjunction with a pediment. Adam was particularly fond of the urn as a decorative motif, and it is constantly found in Neo-Classic furniture. Knife-boxes (q.v.) were often made of urn shape in the late 18th century.

Urn stand
Small 18th-century table designed to carry silver or Sheffield plate tea urns. Usually constructed with a draw slide which pulls out to hold the tea pot.

V

Valance
The hanging drapery around a bedstead, either from the tester or around the frame. The drapery above the top of window curtains.

Varnish
A resinous solution applied to canvas, wood or metal to give a hard, shiny, transparent surface. Also the glaze on pottery. A famous varnish used in French furniture, and subsequently copied in England, was Vernis Martin (q.v.).

Vase
As a motif in furniture, the vase was popular in the Queen Ann period. A vase shape was often used for the central splat in chair-backs.

Veneer
Introduced from Holland in the William and Mary period. A very fine layer of ornamental wood is glued to the surface or carcase of a cheaper wood. The object of the veneer was to give a rich appearance to what was basically an inexpensive piece of furniture. Early veneers were about $\frac{1}{8}$ in. thick, but mechanical cutting in the 19th century reduced the thickness of veneers to about $\frac{1}{50}$ in. and less.

Vernis Martin
A varnish developed in 18th century by Simon-Etienne Martin in imitation of Chinese lacquer. Martin and his two brothers were granted a monopoly of its manufacture in 1730. Widely imitated in England, Vernis Martin gave rise to a considerable production of English and French furniture lacquered in the Oriental manner.

Verres eglomisés
Panels of tinted glass, or foiled glass, commonly used in reliquaries.

Vinaigrette
A small box with a pierced inner lid for holding a sponge

D.A.—E

steeped in aromatic vinegar. Vinaigrettes were usually made of silver, very delicately worked, and were used as smelling bottles. Very popular in both 18th and 19th centuries, they superseded the pomander (q.v.).

Virginal

Square legless spinet used in 16th and 17th centuries. Sometimes harp-shaped, it was keyed and strung for four octaves. Smaller than a spinet, which succeeded it, the virginal was plucked by quills operated from the keyboard.

Vitrine

A French china cabinet with glass sides and doors, often enriched by ormolu mounts and painted or lacquered panels. Widely copied in England during the 'Louis XV' vogue of the late 19th century.

W

Wag-on-the-wall clock

Of Dutch origin, a wall clock with a long exposed pendulum. Weight-driven and found in England towards late 17th century.

Wainscot

Wood panelling. Originally a plain wall panelling of oak. Later developed into elaborate panelling.

Wallpaper

Although crude block-printed paper had been known in England in the 16th century, wallpaper did not become fashionable until it was seen in imported Chinese styles during the 17th century. Printed and painted wallpapers were excellently executed during the 18th century. Commercialised and coarsened in the 19th century, it was revived as a worthwhile decoration by William Morris and his followers.

Walnut

A fine-grained hardwood of rich brown colour. First used widely for furniture in Cromwellian period, but not until

Queen Anne period was walnut fully appreciated. The Age of Walnut lasted for about 100 years and was responsible for the development of the craft of the cabinet-maker. Veneering, marquetry and inlay work also became highly developed. Walnut was finally superseded in fashion by mahogany which dominated the 18th century.

Wardrobe

The wardrobe with its nest of drawers beneath a tall cupboard first appears in the Queen Anne period. It was elaborated and developed during the 18th century by designers such as Chippendale, Hepplewhite and Sheraton.

Warming pan

Possibly of Elizabethan origin and made of brass or copper. The pan, with its lid, was attached to a long handle and was filled with hot coals. Used for airing and warming beds before the advent of the hot-water bottle.

Washstand

Developed in the middle of the 18th century to hold the basin and ewer for washing. Early washstands were usually designed to hold a small pottery basin and had a small drawer in the base for storing soap etc.

Watch

The watch is found in England in Elizabethan times, but was not in general use until much later. Early watches had only an hour hand, the minute hand appearing in the 18th century. Often extremely elaborate, and masterpieces of the goldsmith's and enameller's craft. Watches originally were rather heavy and turnip-shaped, but by the 18th century had evolved into the slim and elegant circle of the typical pocket watch.

Wax polish

Beeswax thinned with turpentine used for polishing furniture and wooden floors.

Web foot

A successor to the club foot (q.v.), rather similar to a flat animal foot. Succeeded in the late 17th century by the claw-and-ball foot.

Wedgwood

Pottery made at the works established by Josiah Wedgwood at Burslem in 1759. The finest pottery ever made in England, Wedgwood ware was of many varieties—Egyptian black ware, Cream ware, Jasper ware, and white biscuit porcelain. In 1769 Josiah Wedgwood took over a second factory which he called Etruria, a name which has ever since been associated with Wedgwood. Jasper ware (q.v.) was perhaps the most famous of all Wedgwood's productions. Marks: Wedgwood, Wedgwood and Bentley (impressed on pottery and stencilled on porcelain); sometimes the word 'Etruria' was added.

Wellington chest

A tall narrow chest of drawers which became popular in the 19th century. Sometimes as many as 12 drawers, all of which can be locked by a hinged wooden flap running right down one side. Used for correspondence and for collections—coins, butterflies, eggs etc.

Welsh dresser

An oak dresser popular in Welsh country districts with pot-board and cupboard. The high top half is occupied by a range of shelves. Some are quite elaborately carved.

Whatnot

A small article rather like a miniature table, but composed of a number of tiers or shelves. Fashionable in the 19th century for the display of china, ornaments etc.

Wheat ear

Ear of wheat used as a design for carving on furniture. Hepplewhite made the wheat ear a fashionable motif.

Wheel back

A chair back, the design of which represents a wheel. Found

in elegant London-made chairs as well as in simple country-made wheel backs.

Wig stand

A toilet stand of the 18th century. It held a basin and glass and was used during the toilet for adjusting the wig. A forerunner of the dressing table and also of the washstand.

William and Mary

1689–1702. The period which saw the revolution in furniture occasioned by the use of walnut, increasing skill of the cabinet-maker and the influx of Continental styles and techniques into England. Cabriole legs, marquetry, veneering, lacquer work, cabinets and bureaux of elegant design, these were but a few of the influences which spread from the furniture of the Court and the nobility down through the country.

Wilton

English town famed for velvet pile carpets. Wilton carpets were at first influenced by Brussels and by Oriental patterns, but later evolved a distinct simple style of their own.

Window seat

Seat specially designed to fit into the window recesses of 18th-century houses. Architect-designers like Adam incorporated such seats into the overall design of a room. Window seats were made by Chippendale and Hepplewhite among others.

Windsor chair

A popular chair with upright lath back and wooden seat. Probably first made near Windsor in the period of Queen Anne. The seat is carved to fit the body, the arm is supported by spindles, as is the back. The back often has a central splat. These country chairs have been popular ever since and are still made. Some elaborate examples had cabriole legs, but mostly the legs are turned and joined by stretchers.

Wine cistern

Fashionable from about mid-17th to mid-18th century and often masterpieces of the silversmith's craft. Not only were they elaborate, but often of vast size, the largest known made by Charles Kandler being capable of holding over 50 gallons.

Wine cooler

Introduced during Carolean period, were usually urn-shaped. Made of silver, but often with zinc or pewter linings to hold the ice. Knife boxes were sometimes incorporated on top of wooden wine coolers which were placed at either end of the side table. These, too, were lined with zinc, lead or pewter.

Wine label

Introduced during the 18th century for hanging on bottles. Made usually of silver, and later enamelled, they were rectangular, oval- or crescent-shaped, and often extremely delicate and decorative.

Wing bookcase

A breakfront type of bookcase with the central section, designed to hold larger volumes, projecting beyond the wings.

Wing chair

A high-backed, upholstered easy chair. Of Carolean origin. The back projected on either side in wings to shield the sitter from draughts. Early examples with needlework upholstery, later upholstered sometimes in leather.

Worcester

Porcelain at the pottery works at Worcester founded 1751. The firm attained fame under the direction of Dr. Wall during the period 1751–1776. After Dr. Wall's death the factory became associated with the names of Flight and Barr. The early period was distinguished by its Oriental designs and by the creamy, slightly greenish tint of the paste. Exotic birds and landscapes with often a royal blue ground. Painting, transfer-printing and line designs printed off copper plates.

Marks: 'W', a Crescent, on early work; numerous marks on later work, but usually incorporating a crown.

Work box
A small box fitted with compartments for cottons, silks, needles etc. Usually of wood and often veneered or inlaid.

Work table

A development of the work box, usually with a tripod support. Later work boxes in the Victorian period became increasingly elaborate, with a silk pouch beneath to hold the silks, wools etc. and a small writing table on top.

Worm holes
Caused in furniture mostly by a type of domestic beetle and its grubs. Long regarded as some evidence of a piece's age, they have been counterfeited in recent years by forgers. Natural worm holes are winding and crooked. Faked wormholes are straight. Worm in antique furniture should be immediately dealt with by a specialist.

X

X-chairs
The most ancient type of chair which evolved from the folding stool. Found in ancient Egypt, Classical Greece and Rome. Made throughout the Middle Ages. The style was revived again in the Renaissance. X-chairs in the 16th century and after were usually highly elaborate and decorative, often used for ecclesiastical furniture in subsequent centuries.

Y

Yew
A very hard, pliable wood, red-brown. Used in country furniture like Windsor chairs and in veneering.

Yorkshire chair

A Commonwealth chair similar to the Lancashire chair, but with an open back. The cross-rails of the back are usually two in number and of semi-circular shape. Usually narrow and plain, only the cross-railings are sometimes relieved by carving.

Z

Zebra wood

A marquetry wood used in the late 18th century. Light brown with prominent dark striped markings. Imported from Guiana.

Some Designers and Makers of Furniture

ADAM BROTHERS—John (1721–1792), Robert (1728–1792), James (1730–1794), and William (1739–1822).

BOULTON, Matthew (b. 1728); manufacturer of mounts for furniture.

CHAMBERS, Sir William (1726–1796); architect and designer.

CHIPPENDALE, Thomas (1718–1779); cabinet-maker: *The Gentleman's and Cabinet Maker's Directory, 1754.* Senior partner in firm of Chippendale, Haig & Co.

CHIPPENDALE, Thomas, Junior (1749–1822); son of Thomas Chippendale.

CIPRIANI, Giovanni (1727–1785); painter and decorator.

COBB, John (d. 1778); cabinet-maker to George III together with William Vile.

COPELAND, H.; furniture designer, c. 1770.

GIBBONS, Grinling (1684–1720); wood-carver and designer.

GILLOW, Robert; cabinet-maker, late 18th century.

HAIG, Thomas; partner of Thomas Chippendale, 1771 to 1796.

HEPPLEWHITE, George (d. 1786); cabinet-maker: The *Cabinet Maker and Upholsterer's Guide* was published in 1788.

INCE, William; cabinet-maker and upholsterer, 18th century.

KAUFFMAN, Angelica (1741–1807); painter who worked with the brothers Adam.

KENT, William (1685–1748); furniture designer and architect.

LANGLEY, Batty and Thomas; designers, 18th century.

LINNELL, John (d. c. 1798); cabinet-maker.

LOCK, Matthias; designer, c. 1752 to 1769.

MANWARING, Robert; cabinet-maker: *The Cabinet and Chair Makers' Real Friend and Companion,* 1765.

MAYHEW, Thomas; partner of William Ince.

PERGOLESI, Michel Angelo; decorator, c. 1760–1800.

SEDDON, George (1727–1801); cabinet-maker.

SHERATON, Thomas (1751–1806); designer: *Cabinet Maker's and Upholsterer's Drawing Book*, 1791–1794.

VILE, WILLIAM (d. 1768); cabinet-maker, worked with John Cobb.

ZUCCHI, Antonio Pietro (1726–1795); worked with Robert Adam. Married Angelica Kauffmann.

Table of the English Periods

The Tudor Period
 Henry VII 1485–1509
 Henry VIII 1509–1547
 Edward VI 1547–1553
 Mary 1553–1558

The Elizabethan Period
 Elizabeth 1558–1603

The Jacobean Period
 James I 1603–1625
 Charles I 1625–1649

The Commonwealth Period
 Cromwell 1649–1660

The Late Stuart or Carolean Period
 Charles II 1660–1685
 James II 1685–1689

The William and Mary Period
 William and Mary 1689–1702

The Queen Anne Period
 Anne 1702–1714
 George I 1714–1727

The Georgian Period
 George II 1727–1760
 George III 1760–1820

The Regency Period
 Strictly speaking, this should cover only the period 1811–1820, when Prince George acted as Regent during his father's madness. It is generally taken to cover the years from 1800 to 1830.
 George IV 1820–1830
 William IV 1830–1837

The Victorian Period
   Victoria   1837–1901

Note

Apart from these dynastic divisions, English furniture of the 18th century is often referred to under the names of famous craftsmen and designers. Thus, the Chippendale period derives its name from the style of furniture produced by, or in emulation of, the cabinet-maker Thomas Chippendale. He was the son of a furniture-maker and wood-carver from Worcestershire and was in business in London from 1749 to 1779. The book of designs which made his name, and which prompted many other craftsmen to follow or improvise upon his style, was called *The Gentleman's and Cabinet Maker's Directory*. It was published in 1754. His son, Thomas Chippendale, carried on his business but went bankrupt in 1805 and died in 1822.

The Hepplewhite period, or style, derives its name from George Hepplewhite who was in business from about 1740 to 1786. The first book of Hepplewhite designs was published two years after his death in 1788, and the firm remained in business until 1805. The Adam Brothers also lent their name to a very distinctive style, although they were not furniture craftsmen so much as architects and designers, who employed others to execute the work for them. Robert, who was the more important of the two, was born in 1728 and died in 1792. Their celebrated book of designs was published in 1775 and exerted a great influence on both furniture and interior decoration. Later, coinciding with the Regency period in England, we find the term 'Empire Period' applied to a great deal of English furniture which was made under the influences of French designers during the life of the Emperor Napoleon Bonaparte.

A List in alphabetical order of some Painters, Sculptors, Engravers, etc.

ABANI, Francesco; painter, 1578–1660.

ABBATE, Niccolo dell'; Italian painter, 1512–1571.

ABBOTT, Francis Lemuel; English portrait painter, 1760–1803.

ABEL, Joseph; German painter of portraits, historical and classical subject, 1768–1818.

ACKERMANN, Johann Adam; German, 1780–1843.

ADAM, Jean Victor; French, 1801–1867.

ADAMS, J. C.; landscape painter, 1840–1906.

ADRIAENSSEN, Alexander; Dutch still-life painter, 1587–1661,

AEKEN, Hieronymus van; known as Jerom Bosch, Dutch, 1462–1518.

AIKMAN, William; Scottish portrait painter, 1682–1731.

ALBANI, Francesco; Italian, 1578–1660.

ALBERELLI, Giacomo; Venetian, 1600–1650.

ALDEGREVER (or Aldegraf), Heinrich; German portrait painter, 1502–1558.

ALDORFER, Albrecht; German painter and engraver, 1480–1538.

ALESSIO, Matteo Perez de; Italian, 1547–c. 1600.

ALKEN, Henry Thomas; engraver, 1785–1851.

ALKEN, Samuel Henry; engraver, 1810–1894.

ALLAN, David; Scottish painter, 1744–1796.

ALLEGRI, Antonio (Correggio); Italian, 1494–1534.

ALLEN, Joseph William; English, 1803–1852.

ALMA-TADEMA, Sir Lawrence, O.M., R.A.; Dutch painter. Settled in England, 1836–1912.

ANDREA D'AGNOLO; known as Andrea del Sarto, Florentine, 1487–1531.

ANGELICO, Fra (Fra Giovanni da Fiesole); Florentine painter, 1387–1455.

ANGELO DI TADDEO GADDI; Italian, 1333–1396.
ANTONIO, Antonello d'; Italian painter, 1420–1493.
ARMITAGE, Edward, R.A.; 1817–1896.
AUDINET, Philippe; engraver, 1766–1837.
AUDUBON, John James; painter of birds, 1780–1851.
AVERCAMP, Hendrik van; Dutch, 1600–?.
BADALOCCHIO, Sisto; Italian, 1581–1647.
BAILY, Edward Hodges, R.A.; 1788–1867.
BAINES, Thomas; 1822–1875.
BALDOVINETTI, Alesso; Florentine, 1427–1499.
BALDUNG, Hans; German, c. 1480–1545.
BALLANTINE, James; Scottish, 1808–1866.
BALLANTYNE, John, R.S.A.; Scottish, 1815–1898.
BANDINELLI, Baccio; Florentine sculptor, 1493–1560.
BANKS, Thomas, R.A.; English sculptor, 1735–1805.
BARBIERI, Giovanni Francesco; Italian, 1591–1666.
BARLOW, Francis; English, 1626–1702.
BARLOW, Thomas Oldham; engraver, 1824–1889.
BARTOLOZZI, Francesco, R.A.; Florentine, 1725–1815.
    Worked mostly in England.
BASSANO, Giacomo da Ponte; Italian, 1510–1592.
BAXTER, George; English engraver, 1805–1867.
BAYNES, James; English painter, 1766–1837.
BEARDSLEY, Aubrey; English black-and-white artist, 1873–
    1898.
BEAUMONT, Sir George Howland; English painter, 1753–1827.
BEAUMONT, John Thomas Barber; miniature painter, 1774–
    1841.
BECK, David; Dutch, 1621–1656.
BEECHEY, Sir William, R.A.; English portrait painter, 1753–
    1839.
BELLINI, Gentile; Venetian painter, 1429–1507.
BELLINI, Giovanni; Venetian painter, c. 1430–1516.
BELLINI, Jacopo; Venetian painter, c. 1400–1470.
BERCHEM, Claes Pietersz; Dutch painter, 1620–1683.
BERNINI, Giovanni Lorenzo; Italian sculptor and painter,
    1598–1680.
BEWICK, Thomas; English engraver, 1753–1838.
BIAGGIO, Bernardino; Italian painter, 1454–1513. Known as
    Pinturicchio.

BIRCH, Charles Bell, A.R.A.; portrait painter, 1832–1893.

BLAKE, William; English painter, 1757–1827.

BODDINGTON, Henry John; English painter, 1811–1865.

BOECKLIN, Arnold; Swiss painter, 1827–1901.

BONE, Henry, R.A.; English painter, 1755–1834.

BONE, Sir Muirhead; painter and engraver, 1876–1953.

BONHEUR, Maria Rosa; French painter, 1822–1899.

BONINGTON, Richard Parkes; English painter, 1801–1828.

BONNARD, Pierre; French painter, 1867–1947.

BOTTICELLI, Sandro; Italian, 1447–1510.

BOUCHER, François; French, 1703–1770.

BOUDIN, Eugene; French, 1842–1898.

BOUGUEREAU, William; French, 1825–1905.

BOYS, Thomas Shotter; English engraver, 1803–1874.

BRABAZON, Hercules B.; English water-colour painter, 1821–1906.

BROUWER, Adrian; Dutch painter, 1605–1638.

BROWN, Charles Armitage; portrait painter, 1786–1842.

BROWN, Ford Madox; English painter, 1821–1893.

BROWNE, Hablot Knight; English black-and-white artist, 1815–1882. ('Phiz'; illustrator of Dickens' works.)

BRUEGHEL, Jan (The Elder); 1568–1625.

BRUEGHEL, Jan (The Younger); 1601–c. 1667.

BRUEGHEL, Peeter (The Younger); 1564–1638.

BRUEGHELL, Peeter (The Elder); 1530–1569.

BRY, Theodor de; Flemish painter and engraver, 1528–1598.

BUONACCORSI, Pietro; Florentine, 1500–1547.

BURNE-JONES, Sir Edward Coley; English, 1833–1898.

BURNEY, E. F.; English portrait painter, 1760–1848.

CALDECOTT, Randolph; English painter, 1846–1886.

CALDERON, Philip Hermogenes, R.A.; English painter, 1833–1898.

CALLCOTT, Sir Augustus Wall; English painter, 1779–1844.

CALLOT, Jacques; French engraver, 1592–1635.

CAMERON, Sir David Young; Scottish painter, 1865–1945.

CANALE, Giovanni Antonio da (Canaletto); Italian, 1698–1768.

CARAVAGGIO, Michelangelo; Italian painter, 1569–1609.

CARPACCIO, Vittore; Venetian, 1479–1522.

CARRACCI, Annibale; Italian painter, 1560–1609.

CASSIE, James; painter, 1819–1879.

CASTIGLIONE, Giovanni; Italian painter, 1616–1670.

CELLINI, Benvenuto; Italian, 1500–1571.

CEZANNE, Paul; French painter, 1839–1906.

CHAGALL, Marc; painter, 1887–.

CHAMBERS, George; English marine painter, 1803–1840.

CHAMPAIGNE, Philippe de; Flemish, 1602–1674.

CHANTREY, Sir Francis Legatt, R.A.; English sculptor and painter, 1781–1842.

CHARDIN, Jean Baptiste Siméon; French painter, 1699–1779.

CHEVANNES, Puvis de; painter, 1824–1898.

CHINNERY, George, R.A.; English painter, 1774–1857.

CHISHOLM, A., R.A.; English painter, 1792–1847.

CIMABUE, Giovanni; Italian, c. 1240–1302.

CIPRIANI, Giovanni Battista; Florentine painter and engraver, 1727–1785.

CLAUDE DE LORRAIN (Clause Gelée); French, 1600–1682.

CLAUSEN, Sir George, R.A.; English painter, 1852–1944.

CLEEF, Jan van; Dutch, 1646–1716.

CLENNEL, Luke; English, 1781–1840.

CLOUET, François; French, 1510–1572.

CLOUET, Jean; French, 1485–1541.

COATES, Samuel; miniature, 1734–1818.

COLLIER, Thomas, R.A.; English painter, 1840–1891.

CONSTABLE, John, R.A.; 1776–1837.

COOKE, Edward William, R.A.; English, 1811–1880.

COOPER, Samuel; miniature, 1609–1672.

COPE, Charles West, R.A.; English, 1811–1880.

COPLEY, John Singleton, R.A.; American, 1737–1815.

CORNELIUS, Peter von; German, 1783–1867.

COROT, Jean Baptiste; French, 1796–1875.

CORREGGIO; see Allegri.

COSWAY, Richard; miniature, 1742–1821.

COTES, Francis, R.A.; English, 1725–1770.

COTMAN, John Sell; English, 1782–1843.

COURBET, Gustave; French, 1819–1877.

COUSIN, Jean; French sculptor and painter, 1500–1589.

COUSINS, Samuel, R.A.; English, 1801–1887.

COX, David; English water-colours, 1809–1885.

COZENS, Alexander; English, 1710–1786.

COZENS, John Robert; English, 1752–1799.

CRANACH, Lucas; German, 1472–1553.
CRANACH, Lucas; German, 1515–1586.
CRANE, Thomas; English, 1808–1859.
CRANE, Walter; English, 1845–1915.
CRESWICK, Thomas, R.A.; English, 1811–1869.
CRIVELLI, Carlo; Venetian, 1430–1493.
CROME, John; English, 1769–1821.
CROME, John Bernay; English, 1794–1842.
CROSSE, Richard; miniatures, 1742–1810.
CRUIKSHANK, George; English engraver, 1792–1878.
CUYP, Aelbert; Dutch, 1620–1691.
CUYP, Jacob; Dutch, 1575–1649.
DANBY, Francis; Irish, 1793–1681.
DANBY, Thomas; landscape painter, fl. 1841–1886.
DANCE, George, R.A.; English, 1741–1825.
DANCE, Nathaniel, R.A.; English, 1734–1811.
DAUBIGNY, Charles François; French, 1817–1878.
DAUMIER, Honoré; French, 1808–1879.
DAVID, Gheeraert; Dutch, 1450–1523.
DAVID, Jacques Louis; French, 1748–1825.
DA VINCI, Leonardo; Florentine, 1452–1519
DAYES, Edward, R.A.; English painter, 1763–1804.
DEGAS, Edgar Hilaire; French, 1834–1917.
DELACROIX, Ferdinand Victor Eugène; French, 1798–1863.
DEL SARTO, Andrea; Florentine, 1486–1531.
DE WINT, Peter; 1784–1849.
DOLCI, Carlo; Florentine, 1616–1686.
DORÉ, Louis; French, 1833–1883.
DOSSO DOSSI, Giovanni; Italian, 1479–1542.
DOU, Gerard; Dutch, 1613–1675.
DOWNMAN, John, A.R.A.; painter, 1750–1824.
DUGDALE, Thomas, R.A.; portrait painter, 1880–1952.
DU MAURIER, George; English caricaturist, 1831–1896.
DURER, Albrecht; German, 1471–1528.
DYCE, William, R.A.; Scottish, 1806–1864.
DYCK, Sir Anthony van; Flemish, 1599–1641.
EAST, Sir Alfred, A.R.A.; English, 1849–1913.
EASTLAKE, Sir Charles Locke, P.R.A.; English, 1793–1865.
EGG, Augustus Leopold, R.A.; English, 1816–1863.
ETTY, William, R.A.; English, 1787–1849.

EYCK, Hubert van; Dutch, 1366–1426.
EYCK, Jan van; Dutch, 1390–1440.
FABRITIUS, Bernhard; Dutch, fl. 1650–1672.
FALCONET, Étienne Maurice; French sculptor, 1716–1791.
FANTIN-LATOUR, I.; French, 1836–1904.
FARINGDON, Joseph, R.A.; painter, 1747–1821.
FARQUARSON, David, A.R.A.; Scottish, 1839–1907.
FARQUHARSON, Joseph, R.A.; Scottish, 1846–1935.
FIELDING, Anthony Vandyke Copley; English, 1788–1855.
FIELDING, Newton Smith; English, 1799–1856.
FIELDING, Theodore; English, 1781–1851.
FILDES, Sir Luke, R.A.; English, 1844–1927.
FISK, William Henry; painter, 1797–1872.
FLANDRIN, Jean Hippolyte; French, 1809–1864.
FLAXMAN, John, R.A.; English, 1755–1826.
FORAIN, Jean Louis; French, 1852–1931.
FOSTER, Myles Birket; painter, 1825–1899.
FOUQUET, Jean (Foucquet); French, 1415–1483.
FRAGONARD, Jean Honoré; French, 1732–1806.
FRAMPTON, Sir George J.; sculptor, 1860–1928.
FRANCESCA, Piero della; Italian, 1420–1492.
FRÈRE, Charles Edouard; painter, 1837–1894.
FULLER, Isaac; painter, 1606–1672.
FURSE, Charles Wellington, A.R.A.; English, 1868–1904.
FUSELI, Johann Heinrich, R.A.; Swiss. Worked in England.
GADDI, Taddeo; Florentine, 1300–1366.
GAINSBOROUGH, Thomas, R.A.; 1727–1788.
GARNIER, Etienne Barthélemy; French, 1759–1849.
GAUGUIN, Paul; painter, 1848–1903.
GEDDES, Andrew, A.R.A.; Scottish, 1783–1844.
GEERAERTS, M.; Flemish, 1561–1635.
GEOFFROY, J.; French, 1853–?
GERARD, François; Italian, 1770–1837.
GERBIER, Sir Balthasar; Dutch, 1592–1667. Worked in England.
GÉRICAULT, Jean Louis André Théodore; French, 1791–1824.
GÉRÔME, Jean Léon; French, 1824–1904.
GHIRLANDAIO, Domenico; Florentine, 1449–1494.
GIBBONS, Grinling; Dutch wood-carver. 1648–1721. Worked in England.

GILBERT, Sir Alfred, R.A.; English sculptor, 1854–1934.
GILBERT, Sir John, R.A.; English painter, 1817–1897.
GILLRAY, James; English caricaturist, 1757–1815.
GILPIN, Sawrey, R.A.; English, 1733–1807.
GIORDANO, Luca (Fa Presto); Italian, 1632–1705.
GIRTIN, Thomas; English water-colourist, 1775–1802.
GODDARD, George Bouverie; painter, 1834–1886.
GOES, Hugo van der; Flemish, 1419–1482.
GOODALL, Edward; English engraver, 1795–1870.
GOODALL, Frederick, R.A.; English painter, 1822–1904.
GOODALL, Walter; English painter, 1830–1889.
GOODWIN, Edward, R.A.; water-colourist, 1801–1808.
GORE, Sir John Watson; painter, 1788–1864.
GORE, Spencer Frederick; painter, 1878–1914.
GOYA y LUCIENTES, Francisco José de; Spanish painter,
    1746–1828.
GOZZOLI, Benozzo; Florentine, 1420–1498.
GRANT, Sir Francis, P.R.A.; Scottish, 1810–1878.
GRAVELOT, Hubert François Bourguignon; French painter,
    1699–1773.
GREEN, Benjamin Richard; painter, 1808–1876.
GREEN, Charles; English water-colourist, 1840–1898.
GREENAWAY, Kate; English illustrator, 1846–1901.
GREUZE, Jean Baptiste; French, 1725–1805.
GRIMALDI, Giovanni Francesco; Italian painter, 1606–1680.
GRIMALDI, William; miniaturist, 1751–1830.
GROSS, Antoine Jean, Baron; French, 1771–1835.
GUARDI, Francesco; Venetian, 1712–1793.
GUÉRIN, Pierre Narcisse, Baron; French, 1774–1833.
GUIDO, R.; Italian painter, 1575–1642.
GUILLAUMIN, Jean Baptiste; French, 1841–1927.
HALS, Frans; Dutch, c. 1580–1666.
HARPIGNIES, H. J.; French, 1819–1916.
HARVEY, Sir George; Scottish, 1806–1876.
HARVEY, William; 1796–1866.
HASSALL, John; engraver, 1767–1825.
HAYDON, Benjamin Robert; English, 1786–1846.
HAYMAN, Francis, R.A.; portrait painter, 1708–1776.
HAYNES, John; painter and engraver, 1760–1829.
HAYTER, Charles; miniaturist, 1761–1835.

HAYTER, Sir George; painter, 1792–1871.
HEIM, François Joseph; French, 1787–1865.
HERKOMER, Sir Hubert von, C.V.O., R.A.; German, 1849–1912. Worked in England.
HERRERA, Francisco de; Spanish, 1576–1656.
HERRING, John Frederick; English, 1795–1865.
HEYDEN, Jan van der; Dutch, 1637–1712.
HIGHMORE, Joseph; English, 1692–1780.
HILL, David Octavius; Scottish, 1802–1870.
HILLIARD, Nicholas; English miniaturist, 1537–1619.
HOARE, Prince; portrait painter, 1775–1834.
HOARE, William, R.A.; English, 1706–1792.
HOBBEMA, Meindert; Dutch, 1638–1709.
HODGES, William, R.A.; English, 1744–1797.
HOGARTH, William; English, 1697–1764.
HOLBEIN, Hans; German, 1460–1524.
HOLBEIN, Hans (the younger); German, 1497–1543.
HOLLOWAY, Thomas; English engraver, 1748–1827.
HOLMAN-HUNT, William, O.M.; English, 1827–1910.
HOMER, Winslow; American, 1836–1910.
HONE, Nathaniel; Irish, 1717–1784.
HOOCH, Pieter de; 1632–c. 1681.
HOPPNER, John, R.A.; English, 1759–1810.
HOUGHTON, Arthur Boyd; English, 1836–1875.
HUBER, Jean; Swiss, 1722–1790.
HUBER, Johann Rudolf; Swiss, 1668–1748.
HUNT, Alfred William; English, 1830–1896.
HUYSUM, Jakob van; Dutch, 1686–1740.
HUYSUM, Jan van; Dutch, 1682–1749.
IBBETSON, Julius Caesar; English, 1759–1817.
INCE, J. M.; 1806–1859.
INCHBOLD, John William, English, 1830–1888.
INGRES, Jean Auguste Dominique, French, 1780–1867.
ISABEY, Eugène L. G.; miniaturist, 1804–1886.
ISABEY, Jean Baptiste; miniaturist, 1767–1855.
JANSSENS, Cornelius; Dutch, 1590–1665.
JOHN, Augustus, R.A.; English, 1878–1961.
JOHN, Gwen; painter, 1876–1939.
JORDAENS, Jacob; Flemish, 1593–1678.
JORDAENS, Jans; Flemish, 1616–1669.

KAUFFMANN, Angelica, R.A.; Swiss painter and engraver, 1741–1807. Worked in England.

KEENE, Charles Samuel; English, 1823–1891.

KENT, William; English, 1684–1748.

KNELLER, Sir Godfrey; German, 1646–1723. Worked in England.

KONINCK, Philipo de; Dutch, 1619–1688.

LA FARGE, John; American, 1835–1910.

LANCRET, Nicolas; French, 1690–1743.

LANDI, Gasparo; painter, 1756–1830.

LANDSEER, Sir Edwin Henry, R.A.; English, 1802–1873.

LANFRANCO, Giovanni; Italian, 1581–1647.

LARGILLIÈRE, Nicolas de; French, 1656–1746.

LAROON, Marcellus; engraver, 1653–1702.

LAURIE, Robert; engraver, 1755–1836.

LAWRENCE, Sir Thomas, P.R.A.; English, 1769–1830.

LEAR, Edward; English, 1812–1888.

LE BLOND, Jean; French, 1635–1709.

LE BRUN, Charles; French, 1619–1690.

LE BRUN, Vigée; French, 1755–1842.

LEECH, John; English, 1817–1864.

LE GROS, Alphonse; French, 1837–1911.

LE GROS, Pierre; French sculptor, 1660–1719.

LEIGHTON, Lord Frederic, P.R.A.; English, 1830–1896.

LELY, Sir Peter; German, 1618–1680. Worked in England.

LEYDEN, Lucas van Jacobsz; Dutch. 1494–1533.

LINNELL, John; painter, 1792–1882.

LINT, Pieter van; Flemish, 1609–1690.

LIPPI, Filippino; Italian, c. 1457–1504.

LIPPI, Fra Filippo; Italian, 1412–1469.

LOTTO, Lorenzo; Venetian, 1480–c. 1555.

LOUTHERBOURG, Phillipe Jacques; French, 1740–1812. Worked in England.

LUCAS, van Leyden; painter, 1494–1533.

LUCIANI, Sebastiano; Venetian, 1485–1547.

LUINI, Bernardino; Italian, 1475–1533.

MABUSE, Jan van; Flemish, 1470–1532.

McEVOY, Ambrose, R.A.; English, 1878–1927.

MACLISE, Daniel, R.A.; Irish, 1806–1870.

MACWHIRTER, John, R.A.; Scottish, 1839–1911.

MAES, Nicholas; Dutch, 1632–1693.

MANET, Edouard; French, 1832–1883.

MANTEGNA, Andrea; Italian, 1431–1506.

MARIS, Jacob; Dutch, 1837–1899.

MARSHALL, Ben; painter, 1767–1835.

MARSHALL, William Calder, R.A.; Scottish, 1813–1894.

MARTIN, John; English, 1789–1854.

MARTINI, Simone; Italian, 1283–1344.

MATSYS, Quentin; Flemish, 1466–c. 1531.

MAUVE, Anton; Dutch, 1838–1888.

MAY, Philip William; English, 1865–1903.

MEDINA, Sir John Baptist; Flemish, 1659–1710. Worked in
    England.

MEISSONIER, Jean Louis Ernest; French, 1815–1891.

MEMLINC, Hans; German, 1430–1494.

MENGS, Ismael Israel; Danish, 1690–1765.

MERCIER, Phillipe; German, 1689–1760. Worked in England.

MESSINA, Antonello Da; Venetian, 1430–1479.

METSU, Gabriel; Dutch, c. 1630–1667.

MEULEN, Adam Frans van der; Flemish, 1632–1690.

MEUNIER, Constantin; Belgian, 1831–1905.

MICHAELANGELO, Buonarrotti; Italian, 1475–1564.

MILLAIS, Sir John Everett, P.R.A.; English, 1829–1896.

MILLET, Jean François; French painter, 1814–1875.

MITCHELL, John; engraver, 1791–1852.

MONET, Claude; French painter, 1840–1926.

MONTAGNA, Bartolommeo; Italian, 1455–1523.

MORE, Sir Anthony (Antoni Moro); painter, 1512–1582.

MOREAU, Jean Michel; French, 1741–1815.

MORISOT, Berthe; French painter, 1840–1895.

MORLAND, George; English painter, 1763–1804.

MORLAND, Henry Robert; painter and engraver, 1730–1797.

MORRIS, William; painter and designer, 1834–1896.

MOSER, Mary, R.A.; flower painter, 1744–1819.

MULREADY, M., R.A.; portrait painter, 1808–1889.

MULREADY, William, R.A.; Irish painter, 1786–1863.

MUNCH, Edvard; Norwegian, 1863–1944.

MUNKACSY, Michel de; Hungarian painter, 1845–1900.

MURILLO, Bartolomé Estéban; Spanish painter, 1618–1682.

MURRAY, Sir David, R.A.; Scottish painter, 1849–1933.

MYTENS, Daniel; Dutch painter, 1590–c. 1656. Worked in England.

NASH, Frederick; water-colourist, 1783–1856.

NASH, Joseph; water-colourist, 1808–1878.

NASH, Paul; English painter, 1889–1946.

NASMYTH, Alexander; Scottish painter, 1758–1840.

NASMYTH, Patrick; Scottish painter, 1787–1831.

NATTIER, Jean Marc; French painter, 1685–1766.

NAVEZ, François Joseph; Belgian painter, 1786–1869.

NETTLESHIP, John Trivett; English painter, 1841–1903.

NEWTON, Francis Milner; painter, 1720–1794.

NEWTON, Gilbert Stuart, R.A.; painter, 1794–1835.

NEWTON, Sir William John; miniaturist, 1785–1869.

NICHOLSON, Sir William; painter, 1872–1949.

NICHOLSON, William; portrait painter, 1784–1844.

NOLLEKENS, Joseph, R.A.; English sculptor, 1737–1823.

NOLLEKENS, Joseph Francis; painter, 1702–1748.

NORTH, John William, A.R.A.; painter, 1824–1924.

NORTHCOTE, James, R.A.; English painter, 1746–1831.

OLIVER, Isaac; English miniaturist, 1556–1617.

OLIVER, Peter; English miniaturist, 1594–1648.

OOST, James van; Flemish painter, 1639–1713.

OPIE, John, R.A.; English portrait painter, 1761–1807.

ORCHARDSON, Sir William Quilter, R.A.; Scottish painter, 1835–1910.

ORPEN, Sir William, R.A.; portait painter, 1878–1931.

OSTADE, Adriaen van; Dutch painter, 1610–1685.

OSTADE, Isack van; Dutch painter, 1621–1649.

OUDRY, Jean Baptiste; French painter, 1686–1755.

OWEN, William, R.A.; portrait painter, 1769–1825.

PALMA, Jacopo (the elder); Italian painter, c. 1480–1528.

PALMA, Jacopo; Italian painter, 1544–1628.

PALMER, Samuel; English water-colourist, 1805–1881.

PARMENTIER, Jacques; painter, 1658–1730.

PARTRIDGE, Sir Bernard; artist and draughtsman, 1861–1945.

PATER, Jean Baptiste Joseph; French painter, 1696–1736.

PATON, Sir Joseph Noel; Scottish painter, 1821–1902.

PATON, Walter Hugh; Scottish painter, 1828–1895.

PAXTON, Sir Joseph; water-colourist, 1801–1865.

PEALE, Charles Wilson; American painter, 1741–1825.

PEALE, Rembrandt; American painter, 1778–1860.

PEETERS, Bonaventura; Flemish painter, 1614–1652.

PENNI, Gianfrancesco; Italian painter, 1488–1528.

PENNI, Luca; 16th-century Italian painter. Worked in England.

PERUGINO, Pietro; painter, 1446–1524.

PERUZZI, Baldassare; Italian painter, 1481–1536.

PETERS, Matthew William; English painter, 1742–1814.

PETRIE, George, P.R.H.A.; Irish painter, 1790–1866.

PETTIE, John, R.A.; Scottish painter, 1839–1893.

PHILIPS, Nathaniel George; English painter and engraver, 1795–1831.

PHILLIP, John, R.A.; Scottish painter, 1817–1867.

PHILLIPS, Thomas, R.A.; English portrait painter, 1770–1845.

PICKERSGILL, Frederick Richard, R.A.; English, 1820–1900.

PICKERSGILL, Henry William, R.A.; painter, 1782–1875.

PIDGEON, Henry Clark; English water-colourist, 1807–1880.

PILLEMENT, Jean; painter, 1727–1808.

PINTURICCHIO, see BIAGGIO

PIOMBO, Fra Sebastiano del; painter, 1485–1547.

PISSARRO, Camille; French painter, 1830–1903.

PLACE, Francis; English painter, 1647–1728.

PLIMER, Andrew; English miniaturist, 1763–1837.

PLIMER, Nathaniel; English miniaturist, 1757–1822.

POLLAIUOLO, Antonio; Florentine sculptor and painter, 1429–1498.

POLLARD, James; engraver, 1797–1859.

POLLARD, Robert; engraver, 1755–1838.

PONTORMO, Jacobo da (Carucci); Italian painter, 1494–1557.

POTTER, Paul; Dutch painter, 1625–1654.

POURBUS, Frans; Flemish painter, 1545–1581.

POURBUS, Pieter; Flemish painter, c. 1510–1584.

POUSSIN, Gaspard Doughet; French painter, 1613–1675.

POUSSIN, Nicolas; French painter, 1594–1665.

POYNTER, Ambrose; water-colour painter, 1796–1886.

POYNTER, Sir Edward Johns, P.R.A.; painter, 1836–1919.

PRINSEP, Valentine Cameron, R.A.; English painter, 1838–1904.

PROUT, John Skinner; water-colourist, 1806–1876.

PROUT, Samuel; water-colourist and etcher, 1783–1852.

PRUD'HON, Pierre Paul; French painter, 1758–1823.

PRYDE, James; painter, 1869–1941.

PUVIS DE CHAVANNES, Pierre Cécile; French painter, 1824–1898.

PYNE, James Baker; painter, 1800–1870.

QUAINI, Luigi; Italian painter, 1643–1717.

QUELLIN, Erasmus; Flemish sculptor and painter, 1607–1678.

QUELLYN, Artus; Flemish sculptor and painter, 1630–1715.

RAE, Henrietta; English painter, 1859–1928.

RAEBURN, Sir Henry, R.A.; Scottish painter, 1756–1823.

RAMSAY, Allan; Scottish painter, 1713–1784.

RAMSAY, James; painter, 1786–1854.

RAPHAEL (Raffaello SANZIO); Italian painter, 1483–1520.

RAVESTEYN, Jan van; Dutch painter, 1580–1665.

READ, David Charles; painter and etcher, 1790–1851.

REDOUTE, P. J.; flower painter, 1759–1840.

REID, Sir George, P.R.S.A.; painter, 1841–1913.

REID, J.; Scottish painter, 1851–1926.

REINAGLE, Philip, R.A.; English painter, 1749–1833.

REINAGLE, Ramsay Richard, R.A.; painter, 1775–1862.

REMBRANDT, van Ryn, Harmensz; Dutch, 1606–1669.

RENI, Guido; Italian painter, 1575–1642.

RENOIR, Pierre-Auguste; French painter, 1841–1919.

REYNOLDS, Sir Joshua, P.R.A.; English painter, 1723–1792.

REYNOLDS, Samuel William; English painter and engraver, 1773–1835.

REYNOLDS, Samuel William; English painter and engraver, 1794–1872.

RIBALTA, Francesco de; Spanish painter, 1551–1628.

RIBERA, Jose de; Spanish painter, 1588–1656.

RIBOT, Augustin T.; French painter and engraver, 1823–1891.

RICCI, Sebastiano (Rizzi); Venetian painter, 1659–1734. Worked in England.

RICCIO, David; painter, 1494–1567.

RICHARDSON, Jonathan; painter, 1665–1745.

RICHARDSON, Thomas Miles; landscape painter, 1784–1848.

RICHARDSON, Thomas Miles (Junior); painter and engraver, 1813–1890.

RIGAUD Y ROS, Hyacinthe; French painter, 1659–1743.

ROBERT, Hubert; painter, 1733–1808.

ROBERT-FLEURY, Joseph Nicolas; French genre painter, 1798–1891.

ROBERTS, David, R.A.; Scottish painter, 1796–1864.

ROBERTSON, Alexander; Scottish painter and miniaturist, 1772–1841.

ROBERTSON, Andrew; Scottish painter and miniaturist, 1777–1845.

ROBERTSON, Archibald; Scottish painter and miniaturist, 1765–1835.

ROBUSTI, Jacopo (Tintoretto); Venetian painter, 1518–1594.

RODIN, Auguste; French sculptor, 1840–1917.

ROMANELLI, Giovanni Francesco; Italian painter, 1610–1662.

ROMNEY, George; English painter, 1734–1802.

ROOKER, Michael Angelo; water-colourist and engraver, 1743–1801.

ROOS, Johann Heinrich; Dutch painter and engraver, 1631–1685.

ROOS, Joseph; landscape painter, 1728–1805.

ROOS, Philipp Peter; German painter, 1657–1705.

ROSA, Salvatore; Italian painter, 1615–1673.

ROSSETTI, Gabriel Charles Dante; English painter, 1828–1882.

ROSSI, Francesco (il Salviati); Italian painter, 1510–1563.

ROSSI, Giovambattista dei; Florentine painter, 1494–1541.

ROUSSEAU, Pierre Étienne Theódore; French painter, 1812–1867.

ROWLANDSON, Thomas; English water-colourist, 1756–1827.

RUBENS, Sir Peter Paul; Flemish painter, 1577–1640.

RUSKIN, John; painter and critic, 1819–1900.

RUYSDAEL, Salomon van; Dutch painter, 1670.

SABBATINI, Andrea (da Salerno); Italian painter, c. 1480–1545.

SABBATINI, Lorenzo; Italian painter, c. 1530–1577.

SALVATOR, Rosa; painter, 1615–1673.

SANDBY, Paul, R.A.; English painter, 1725–1809.

SANDBY, Thomas, R.A.; water-colourist, 1721–1798.

SANTERRE, Jean Baptiste; painter, 1658–1717.

SANZIO, Raffaello (Raphael); Italian painter, 1483–1520.

SARGENT, John Singer, R.A.; painter, 1856–1925.

SARTORIOUS, Francis; animal painter, 1734–1804.

SARTORIOUS, J. N.; sporting painter, 1755–1828.

SCOTT, David; Scottish painter, 1806–1849.

SEURAT, Georges; French painter, 1859–1890.

SEVERN, Joseph, R.A.; painter, 1793–1879.

SHAW, J. Byam; draughtsman, 1872–1919.

SHEE, Sir Martin Archer, P.R.A.; Irish portrait painter, 1769–1850.

SICKERT, Walter Richard, A.R.A.; English painter, 1860–1942.

SIGNAC, Paul; French painter, 1863–1935.

SIMPSON, William; Scottish painter, 1823–1899.

SISLEY, Alfred; painter, 1839–1899.

SMART, John; Scottish painter, 1839–1899.

SMART, John; English miniaturist, 1741–1811.

SMITH, Colvin; portrait painter, 1795–1875.

SMITH, Frederick William; sculptor, 1797–1835.

SNYDERS, Frans; Dutch painter, 1579–1657.

STANFIELD, George Clarkson; painter, 1828–1878.

STANFIELD, William Clarkson, R.A.; English painter, 1793–1867.

STANNARD, Joseph; painter, 1797–1830.

STEEN, Jan; Dutch painter, 1626–1679.

STEER, Philip Wilson; painter, 1860–1942.

STEVENS, Alfred; English sculptor and painter, 1817–1875.

STONE, Marcus, R.A.; English genre painter, 1840–1921.

STOTHARD, Thomas, R.A.; English painter, 1755–1834.

STOTT, Wm., R.A.; English painter, 1858–1900.

STUBBS, George; English animal painter, 1724–1806.

TENIERS, David (the elder); Flemish painter, 1582–1649.

TENIERS, David (the younger); Flemish painter, 1610–1690.

TER BORCH, Gerard; Dutch painter, 1617–1681.

THORNHILL, Sir James; English painter, 1675–1734.

THORVALDSEN, Bertel; Danish sculptor, 1770–1844.

TIEPOLO, Giovanni Battista; Italian painter, 1696–1769.

TINTORETTO (Jacopo ROBUSTI); Venetian painter, 1518–1594.

TISCHBEIN, Johann Heinrich; German painter, 1722–1789.

TISCHBEIN, Johann Heinrich Wilhelm; German painter, 1751–1829.

TISSOT, James Joseph Jacques; French water-colourist, 1836–1902.

TITIAN (Tiziano Vecelli); Venetian painter, 1477–1576.
TOULOUSE-LAUTREC, Henri de; painter, 1864–1902.
TOWNE, Francis; landscape painter, 1740–1816.
TROYON, Constant; French painter, 1810–1865.
TURNER, Joseph Mallord William, R.A.; English painter, 1775–1851.
UBERTINI, Francesco (Il Bachiacca); 1494–1557.
UDEN, Lucas van; Flemish painter, 1595–1673.
VALDES-LEAL, Juan de; Spanish painter, 1630–1691.
VANDERVELDE, Wilem ('The Old'); Dutch painter, 1610–1693.
VANDERVELDE, Wilem; Dutch marine painter, 1633–1707.
VAN DYKE, Sir Anthony; painter, 1599–1641.
VAN EYCK, Hubert; painter, 1366–1426.
VAN GOGH, Vincent; Dutch painter, 1853–1890.
VAN LOO, Charles André; painter, 1705–1765.
VAN LOO, Jean Baptiste; painter, 1684–1745.
VANNUCCI, Pietro (Perugino); Italian painter, 1446–1524.
VAN OS, Pieter Gerard; painter, 1776–1839.
VAN OSTADE, Adraen; painter, 1620–1685.
VAN OSTADE, Isaak; painter, 1621–1649.
VARGAS, Luis de; Spanish religious painter, 1502–1568.
VARLEY, Cornelius; English water-colourist, 1781–1873.
VARLEY, John; English water-colourist, 1778–1842.
VASARI, Giorgio; Italian painter, 1512–1574.
VEEN, Maerten van (Heemskerk); Dutch painter, 1498–1574.
VELAZQUEZ DE SILVA, Diego; Spanish painter, 1599–1660.
VELDE, Adriaen van; Dutch painter, 1635–1672.
VERMEER, Jan (Van de Meer); Dutch painter, 1632–1675.
VERNET, Antoine Charles Horace; French painter, 1758–1836.
VERNET, Claude Joseph; French painter, 1714–1789.
VERROCCHIO, Andrea del; Florentine painter, 1435–1488.
VINCI, Leonardo da; Italian, 1452–1519.
VOS, Cornelis de; Flemish painter, 1585–1651.
VOS, Simon de; Flemish painter, 1603–1676.
VOUET, Simon; French painter, 1590–1649.
VUILLARD, Jean Edouard; painter, 1868–1940.
WARD, Edward Matthew, R.A.; English painter, 1816–1879.
WARD, James, R.A.; English painter, 1769–1859.
WATTEAU, Jean Antoine; French painter, 1684–1721.

WATTS, George Frederick, O.M., R.A.; English sculptor and painter, 1817–1904.

WEEKES, Henry, R.A.; English sculptor, 1807–1877.

WEENIX, Jan; Dutch painter, 1640–1719.

WEST, Benjamin, P.R.A.; American painter, 1739–1820. Worked in England.

WESTALL, Richard; English painter, 1765–1836.

WESTMACOTT, Sir Richard; English sculptor, 1775–1856.

WESTMACOTT, Richard, R.A.; English sculptor, 1779–1872.

WEYDEN, Rogier van der; French painter, 1399–1464.

WHEATLEY, Francis, R.A.; English painter, 1747–1801.

WHISTLER, James Abbott McNeill; American painter, 1834–1903. Worked in England.

WILKIE, Sir David, R.A.; Scottish painter, 1785–1841.

WILSON, Richard, R.A.; English painter, 1714–1782.

WINCKELMANN, F. X.; German painter, 1806–1873.

WINT, Peter de; English water-colourist, 1784–1849.

WINTERHALTER, Franz Xaver; painter, 1806–1873.

WIT, Jacob de; Dutch painter, 1695–1754.

WITTE, Emanuel de; Dutch painter, 1607–1692.

WOLSTENHOLME, Dean; English painter, 1757–1837.

WOODFORDE, Samuel, R.A.; painter, 1763–1817.

WOOLNER, Thomas, R.A.; portrait painter, 1825–1892.

WOUVERMANS, Jan; Dutch painter, 1629–1666.

WOUVERMANS, Philip; Dutch painter, 1619–1668.

WRIGHT, Joseph, R.A.; English painter, 1734–1798.

WYATT, Henry; painter, 1794–1840.

WYATT, Matthew Cotes; English sculptor, 1777–1862.

WYATT, Richard James; English sculptor, 1793–1850.

WYNANTS, Jan; Dutch landscape painter, 1615–1682.

ZAMPIERI, Domenico (Domenichino); Italian painter, 1581–1641.

ZOFFANY, Johann, R.A.; German painter, 1733–1810. Worked in England.

ZUCCARELLI, Francesco, R.A.; Italian painter, 1702–1788. Worked in England.

ZUCCARO (Zuccharo), Federigo; Italian painter, 1542–1609.

ZUCCARO (Zuccharo), Taddeo; Italian painter, 1529–1566.

ZURBARAN, Francisco de; Spanish painter, 1598–1662.

ADVERTISING & PUBLICITY   ALGEBRA   AMATEUR ACTING   ANAT
BOOK-KEEPING   BRICKWORK   BRINGING UP CHILDREN   BUSINE
CHESS   CHINESE   COMMERCIAL ARITHMETIC   COMMERCIAL AR
COMPOSE MUSIC   CONSTRUCTIONAL DETAILS   CONTRACT BRIDGE
SPEEDWORDS   ECONOMIC GEOGRAPHY   ECONOMICS   ELECTR
ENGLISH GRAMMAR   LITERARY APPRECIATION   ENGLISH RENASC
REVIVAL   VICTORIAN AGE   CONTEMPORARY LITERATURE   ETCHI
FREELANCE WRITING   FRENCH   FRENCH DICTIONARY   FRENCH
LIVING THINGS   GEOLOGY   GEOMETRY   GERMAN   GERMAN
GOOD CONTROL OF INSECT PESTS   GOOD CONTROL OF PLANT DISEA
GOOD FARMING BY MACHINE   GOOD FARM WORKMANSHIP   GOO
GOOD MARKET GARDENING   GOOD MILK FARMING   GOOD PIG KE
GOOD ENGLISH   GREEK   GREGG SHORTHAND   GUIDEBOOK TO T
GREAT BOLIVAR   BOTHA   CATHERINE THE GREAT   CHATHAM   CLE
LIBERALISM   HENRY V   JOAN OF ARC   JOHN WYCLIFFE   LENIN   LOUIS
ROBES   HASTINGS
HOUS   REPAIRS
WRITE   ND TOO
MECH   LCRAFT
MOTO   FICIENC
PHYSIC   DESIGN
ADMI   RE
PHR   BOOK   SAILING   SALESMANSHIP   SECRETA   ACTICE
DEBATE   SPELLING   STAMP COLLECTING   STUDE   DE   ST
TYPEWRITING   USE OF GEOGRAPHY   WAY TO POETR   WRI
COOKERY FOR GIRLS   DOGS AS PETS FOR BOYS AND GIRLS   KNIT
PHOTOGRAPHY FOR BOYS AND GIRLS   RADIO FOR BOYS   RIDING
SOCCER FOR BOYS   STAMP COLLECTING FOR BOYS AND GIRLS   WO
ACTING   ANATOMY   ARABIC   ASTRONOMY   BANKING   BE
CHILDREN   BUSINESS ORGANISATION   CALCULUS   CANASTA   C
COMMERCIAL ART   COMMERCIAL CORRESPONDENCE   COMMER
CONTRACT BRIDGE   COOKING   CRICKET   DRAWING   DRESS
ECONOMICS   ELECTRICITY   ELECTRICITY IN THE HOUSE   ELOCU
ENGLISH RENASCENCE   ENGLISH RENASCENCE TO THE ROMANTIC
LITERATURE   ETCHING   EVERYDAY FRENCH   TO EXPRESS YOURS
DICTIONARY   FRENCH PHRASE BOOK   GARDENING   GAS IN T
GERMAN   GERMAN DICTIONARY   GERMAN GRAMMAR   GERMAN
CONTROL OF PLANT DISEASES   GOOD FARM ACCOUNTING   G
GOOD FARM WORKMANSHIP   GOOD FRUIT FARMING   GOOD GRA
GOOD MILK FARMING   GOOD PIG KEEPING   GOOD POULTRY KEE
GREGG SHORTHAND   GUIDEBOOK TO THE BIBLE   HINDUSTANI
CATHERINE THE GREAT   CHATHAM   CLEMENCEAU   CONSTANTINE CO
ARC   JOHN WYCLIFFE   LENIN   LOUIS XIV   MILTON   PERICLES   PETER
USE OF HISTORY   WARREN HASTINGS   WOODROW WILSON   HOCKE
HOUSEHOLD ELECTRICITY   HOUSE REPAIRS   ITALIAN   JOINERY
MANAGEMENT   MATHEMATICS   HAND TOOLS   ENGINEERING
DRAUGHTSMANSHIP   METEOROLOGY   MODELCRAFT   MODERN DA
MUSIC   NORWEGIAN   PERSONAL EFFICIENCY   PHILOSOPHY   PHO
SHORTHAND   PLANNING AND DESIGN   PLUMBING   POLISH   PO

GIVE INSTRUCTION TO A WISE MAN···